P9-AQW-202

BEST OF

Athens

Victoria Kyriakopoulos

How to use this book

Colour-Coding & Maps

Each chapter has a colour code along the banner at the top of the page which is also used for text and symbols on maps (eg all venues reviewed in the Highlights chapter are orange on the maps). The fold-out maps inside the front and back covers are numbered from 1 to 11. All sights and venues in the text have map references; eg, (11, C2) means Map 11, grid reference C2. See p128 for map symbols.

Prices

Multiple prices listed with reviews (eg [€10/5]) usually indicate adult/concession admission to a venue. Concession prices can include senior, student, member or coupon discounts. Meal cost and room rate categories are listed at the start of the Eating and Sleeping chapters, respectively.

Text Symbols

- ☎ telephone
- ✉ address
- 🖥 email/website address
- € admission
- ◷ opening hours
- ⓘ information
- Ⓜ metro
- 🚌 bus
- 🚋 trolley
- 🚗 car
- ⛴ ferry
- ♿ wheelchair access
- ✕ on-site/nearby eatery
- 🧒 child-friendly venue

Best of Athens
3rd edition – March 2007
First published – May 2002

Published by Lonely Planet Publications Pty Ltd
ABN 36 005 607 983

Australia Head Office, Locked Bag 1, Footscray, Vic 3011
☎ 03 8379 8000, fax 03 8379 8111
🖥 talk2us@lonelyplanet.com.au
USA 150 Linden St, Oakland, CA 94607
☎ 510 893 8555, toll free 800 275 8555
fax 510 893 8572
🖥 info@lonelyplanet.com
UK 72–82 Rosebery Ave, Clerkenwell, London
EC1R 4RW
☎ 020 7841 9000, fax 020 7841 9001
🖥 go@lonelyplanet.co.uk

This title was commissioned in Lonely Planet's London office and produced by: **Commissioning Editor** Stefanie Di Trocchio **Coordinating Editors** Maryanne Netto & Kyla Gillzan **Coordinating Cartographer** Erin McManus **Layout Designer** Jim Hsu **Cartographer** Ross Butler **Managing Cartographer** Mark Griffiths **Project Manager** Rachel Imeson **Mapping Development** Paul Piaia **Desktop Publishing Support** Mark Germanchis **Thanks to** Sally Darmody, Katie Lynch, Kate McDonald, Celia Wood

Photographs by Lonely Planet Images and Anders Blomqvist except for the following: p79 (#1, #2) Alan Benson; p52 Mark Daffey; p50 Paul David Hellander; p48 John Elk III; p28 Lou Jones; p92 Izzet Keribar; p50 Diana Mayfield; p5 Aliki Sapountzi; p8, p14, p20 (#1, #2), p36, p37, p66, p70, p78, p80, p81, p82, p83, p84, p87, p103, p104, p111 Neil Setchfield; p42 Jan Stromme. **Cover photograph** Ruins of Islamic school near the Roman Agora, Peter Grumann/Photolibrary. All images are copyright of the photographers unless otherwise indicated. Many of the images in this guide are available for licensing from Lonely Planet Images: www.lonelyplanetimages.com.

ISBN 9 78174 059 8118

Printed through Colorcraft Ltd, Hong Kong.
Printed in China

Contents

From the Publisher

AUTHOR
Victoria Kyriakopoulos

When not living her 'other life' in Greece, Victoria Kyriakopoulos is a freelance journalist based in Melbourne, Australia. A regular visitor to Athens since 1988, she lived there between 2000 and 2004, witnessing and reporting on the city's angst-ridden pre-Olympic makeover.

Like most Athenians, she learnt to accept and enjoy the city's quirky and chaotic nature, helped along by a good sense of humour, healthy cynicism, increased as-sertiveness and occasional frustrated outbursts.

While she concedes that Athens can be a love it or hate it place, she is keen to ensure visitors are equipped to discover its often hidden charms and decide for themselves.

During her time in Athens, she was editor of the Athens-based Greek diaspora magazine *Odyssey*, a regular contributor to the *Age, Sydney Morning Herald* and other Australian and international publications, and a TV researcher. Victoria wrote the previous editions of Lonely Planet's *Athens Condensed* and *Best of Athens* and updated the 3rd edition of *Crete*, as well as the Athens chapter of *Greece 7*.

In her hometown of Melbourne, she's had various career incarnations, including stints as a staff writer with the *Bulletin*, columnist for the *Age* newspaper, government press secretary, and reporter on the *Melbourne Herald*.

Thanks to Xenia Orfanos, Lefteris Stavropoulos, Vicky Valanos, Antonis Bekiaris, Eleni Bertes, Mary Retiniotis, Eleni Gialama, Theoni Mavroidakou, Fiona Hattersley-Smith, Athina Vorilla, Carlos Van Meek, Marianna Kostara and Chris Anastassiades.

LONELY PLANET AUTHORS

Why is our travel information the best in the world? It's simple: our authors are independent, dedicated travellers. They don't research using just the internet or phone, and they don't take freebies in exchange for positive coverage. They travel widely, to all the popular spots and off the beaten track. They personally visit thousands of hotels, restaurants, cafés, bars, galleries, palaces, museums and more – and they take pride in getting all the details right, and telling it how it is. For more, see the authors section on **www.lonelyplanet.com**.

PHOTOGRAPHER
Anders Blomqvist

Originally from Sweden, but now considering himself a citizen of Planet Earth, Anders Blomqvist has travelled the world for over 25 years in pursuit of a good time and great photos. He has worked on a luxury liner, and for over 10 years as a trekking and rafting guide in Nepal, Tibet, Norway and Australia.

He now divides his time between a small coastal village in southern Sweden, and Asia or the Middle East.

SEND US YOUR FEEDBACK

We love to hear from travellers – your comments keep us on our toes and help make our books better. Our well-travelled team reads every word on what you loved or loathed about this book. Although we cannot reply individually to postal submissions, we always guarantee that your feedback goes straight to the appropriate authors, in time for the next edition – and the most useful submissions are rewarded with a free book. To send us your updates – and find out about Lonely Planet events, newsletters and travel news – visit our award-winning website: **www.lonelyplanet.com/feedback**.

Note: We may edit, reproduce and incorporate your comments in Lonely Planet products such as guidebooks, websites and digital products, so let us know if you don't want your comments reproduced or your name acknowledged. For a copy of our privacy policy visit www.lonelyplanet.com/privacy.

Introducing Athens

For so long, modern Athens lived in the shadow of its glorious past, the awe-inspiring Acropolis rising defiant over the sprawling, chaotic concrete metropolis below. It promised us a miracle for the 2004 Olympics and no one can deny the extraordinary transformation the city finally unveiled.

The historic centre is unrecognisable since cars were banished and significant archaeological sites linked in what has become Europe's longest, and arguably most stunning, pedestrian promenades. This huge archaeological park reconciles past and present, with the city's cultural and social life taking place around ancient monuments.

The city's renaissance includes a new airport, a modern metro and efficient public transport, new shopping and entertainment precincts, more open, green spaces, and a renewal of run-down urban areas.

Athens has a new buzz and visitors to the Greek capital will be pleasantly surprised by the diverse experiences the city offers, from history and culture to lively nightlife. Almost year-round sunshine, the seasonal dynamics of Athenian life and the close proximity of major sights and entertainment options add to Athens' appeal as a destination to head for any time of the year, rather than a quick stopover en route to the islands.

Athens is still a work in progress and a city full of contradictions. Much of its charm lies beyond the façade, in its vibrant street life, quirky energy and somewhat anarchistic and laid-back nature. Athenians are social animals, taking time out for endless coffees and evening strolls, dining out until late and enjoying the nightlife. There's certainly something oddly life-affirming about 3am traffic, while pink evening skies over the Acropolis and walks through the historic centre never fail to impress.

The Agora in the Olympic Sports Complex (p38) is an integral part of the modern-day city

Neighbourhoods

Downtown Athens and the revitalised historic neighbourhoods under the Acropolis are where visitors spend most of their time. The city's major sights, art and entertainment precincts are now virtually all within a linked pedestrian precinct (p15), making Athens an easy city to explore.

Beyond the usual tourist trail, Athens has many interesting neighbourhoods, each with its unique character and insight into the spectrum of modern Athenian life.

Syntagma Sq (Platei Syntagmatos; Constitution Sq), dominated by Parliament, is the heart of modern Athens, the hub of its political life, business district and shopping precincts.

Overrun by tourists in summer, **Plaka** nonetheless retains its charm. Locals still come to the old quarter's tavernas and cafés, making it lively year-round. While many traditional stores have been replaced by souvenir and jewellery stores, you can wander off the tourist strip and get a glimpse of old Athens.

Walk down Syntagma Sq to Parliament (p16)

Monastiraki is not as grungy as it used to be, but still has a curious mix of stores, the flea market, its renowned souvlaki precinct and quirky corners such as Plateia Avyssinias. Stores along the pedestrian route have been spruced up and many new cafés and restaurants have livened up the area.

Next to Monastiraki, **Psiri**, the 'Soho' of Athens has a deceptively seedy façade. It is bustling at night with people enjoying the theatres, restaurants, bars and clubs that have almost engulfed this newly fashionable district, sending many of its original bohemians scurrying elsewhere. Psiri's live music tavernas have a tradition of merry late

Sunday afternoons, while slick warehouse conversions, restored neoclassical houses, hip galleries and stores now compete with an offbeat mix of old stores, bakeries and workshops.

The pedestrian walk around the Acropolis has made **Thisio** blossom, and drawn people to its new galleries, cafés and bars, largely concentrated on the main promenade and Iraklidon.

From Thisio, pedestrian Ermou leads to the once semi-industrial area of **Gazi,** whose revival started with the transformation of the historic gasworks into the Technopolis cultural centre (p39). Its illuminated red chimneys are like a beacon around which trendy restaurants, bars and nightclubs have sprouted – and these are spreading to nearby **Rouf**. Gazi has become the hub of gay Athens.

Despite valiant clean-up efforts and the arrival of some funky hotels, most of the areas around **Omonia** retain their seedy character. It is also the hub of an emerging ethnic quarter, where Athens' many migrants congregate.

In total contrast, elite **Kolonaki** is the most classy – and flashy – neighbourhood of central Athens. From the main square, with its busy people-watching cafés, the streets leading up **Lykavittos Hill** are full of chic boutiques, restaurants and galleries.

Kolonaki's lively bohemian neighbour, **Exarhia**, has a more earthy character. Although partly gentrified, particularly heading up towards Strefi Hill, it's popular with students (it's near the universities), artists and left-wing intellectuals due to its historic association with radical politics and the junta-era. It has good-value tavernas and many alternative book, music and clothing stores and *rebetika* clubs (clubs playing the Greek version of the blues).

The smart seaside suburb of **Glyfada** was once a resort town and every summer it draws people to its beaches, beach bars, clubs and restaurants. It also has great shopping. The scenic tram to Glyfada has given the area a boost after the demise of the old airport.

Leafy **Kifisia** was once a cool northern retreat, where rich Athenians had their villas. It is now more of an elegant upmarket suburb with great bars, restaurants and shopping. The mansions and tree-lined streets and gardens are a far cry from the urban centre.

Beyond its function as the main port of Athens, **Piraeus** is a bustling, chaotic and interesting city in its own right. While there are few sights, it has its charms, particularly the coastal promenade around its harbours, including picturesque Mikrolimano, lined with waterfront cafés, bars and restaurants.

> **OFF THE BEATEN TRACK**
> To get away from the tourist bustle, you can't go wrong with a drive up to the hills to the Kaisariani Monastery (p34). Closer to town, the ancient cemetery of Athens at Keramikos (p27) is one of the more peaceful and less-frequented archaeological sites and Strefi Hill (left) near Exarhia offers a different outlook on Athens. Alternatively, venture outside Athens to the Koutouki Cave (p42) and Vorres Museum (p43).

Grand Lykavittos Hill (p20) rising above Athens' urban sprawl

Itineraries

Ancient Athens was tiny compared to the sprawling metropolis of today. Visitors need not be intimidated though. The historic centre, important archaeological sites, major landmarks, museums and attractions are concentrated in the centre and within walking distance of each other. This makes Athens a great walking city, with loads of nooks and interesting neighbourhoods to explore.

In summer, it is best to see the archaeological sites early in the morning and spend the hottest part of the day at a cool museum. The Acropolis and major sights stay open until about 7.30pm in summer so the alternative is to head there in the late afternoon, which avoids the tour groups. Many smaller sites and state-run museums, however, close by 2pm (for museum costs and opening hours see p29).

Wear rubber-soled shoes as the ancient marble surfaces can be very slippery and uneven.

In summer you can also take a break from the urban centre and head to the beach for a swim or your evening entertainment.

Winter offers quite a different set of experiences, so factor the season into your itinerary.

DAY ONE

Head to the **Acropolis** (p10), Athens' crowning jewel, and wind your way down through the **Ancient Agora** (p17) to the streets of Plaka for lunch at one of its atmospheric tavernas. Take a walk through the **Roman Agora** (p18) and visit the **Turkish Baths** (p33) before browsing through the **Monastiraki Flea Market** (p54) and making your way to Thisio for coffee along the pedestrian promenade. Squeeze in a walk to **Keramikos** (p27), before an afternoon rest. For dinner, choose a restaurant in **Plaka** (p70) or **Thisio** (p69), where you can dine under the floodlit Acropolis. Kick on to **Psiri** (p90) for a drink at one of the area's many bars, catch some live Greek music or go clubbing.

DAY TWO

Catch the changing of the guard ceremony at **Parliament** (p16) in Syntagma before heading to the **National Archaeological Museum** (p14) to explore Greece's most significant collection of antiquities. Do some window

Something to light up anyone's room at the Monastiraki Flea Market (p54)

WORST OF ATHENS

A few things that can stress you out in Athens:

- Traffic, noise and Athens' drivers
- Pavements that can be uneven, potholed and treacherous
- The small but nasty percentage of rip-off taxi drivers
- Having to yell to hail a speeding taxi in peak hour
- The early closing hours of some sights
- Strikes by taxis and archaeological-site employees
- Inflated prices, especially for coffee and drinks

shopping in Kolonaki or people-watching at its trendy cafés, before heading to the **Benaki Museum** (p19), where you can lunch on the rooftop overlooking the National Gardens. Stroll down to the old **Panathenaic Stadium** (p39) and then to the **Temple of Olympian Zeus** (p25) and **Hadrian's Arch** (p25). In the evening, grab a quick souvlaki at **Monastiraki** (p70) before catching a show at the historic **Odeon of Herodes Atticus** (p26), ending the evening with a leisurely stroll along the pedestrian promenade and a nightcap at one of the cafés under the Acropolis. Alternatively, take the funicular railway up **Lykavittos Hill** (p20) at sunset for impressive panoramic views of Athens, then dine at a traditional taverna with a courtyard garden or rooftop terrace.

DAY THREE

Take a peaceful, car-free early morning walk up to **Filopappou Hill** and the **Hill of the Pnyx** (see our do-it-yourself walking tour, p47) for breathtaking views of the city. Visit the **Museum of Cycladic & Ancient Greek Art** (p21), the **Byzantine & Christian Museum** (p24) or the **National Art Gallery** (p22). Have lunch in the tavernas around the **Athens Central Market** (p54), before heading off for some shopping in Plaka or Ermou.

In the evening head to **Gazi** for dinner and some bar-hopping (p88) or skip the bars and cab it to some live Greek music at a *rebetika* club (a club playing the Greek equivalent of the blues), or explore the busy live-music scene.

Get cultured at the Benaki Museum (p19)

In summer consider heading to the waterfront. Take the tram to one of the beachfront restaurants along the coast towards **Glyfada** (p79), where you can later kick on at one of the busy summer clubs (p91). Alternatively, head to Piraeus for a seafood dinner in **Mikrolimano** (p78) by the harbour, followed by a drink at one of the nearby bars (p91).

Highlights

ACROPOLIS (11, A3)

Even when you live in Athens, the magnificent sight of the Acropolis standing defiant and dignified over Athens never fails to impress. Time, war, pilfering, earthquakes and pollution have taken their toll on the sacred hill and its crowning glory, the Parthenon – the most important ancient monument in the Western world.

First inhabited in Neolithic times, the Acropolis served as a fortress, a place of cult worship, and it is believed there was a Mycenaean palace on the peak. Many temples were built on the Acropolis (High City) paying homage to the goddess Athena.

INFORMATION

- ☎ 210 321 0219
- 🖳 www.culture.gr
- ✉ Acropolis (main entrance from Dionysiou Areopagitou or Theorias or use the Theatre of Dionysos entrance if you aren't carrying large bags)
- € €12 (valid 4 days & includes entrance to Roman & Ancient Agoras, Keramikos, Temple of Olympian Zeus & Dionysos Theatre)
- ⏱ 8am-7.30pm (8am-5pm Nov-Mar)
- ℹ opens once a year in August for full moon, see papers for listings
- Ⓜ Akropoli
- ♿ good access to some parts of site via lift and special walkways

The buildings were destroyed by the Persians in 480 BC. Following this, Pericles transformed the Acropolis into a magnificent city of temples that has come to be regarded as the zenith of classical Greek achievement.

In subsequent years, this area served as the military stronghold for successive occupiers, with the buildings converted into Christian churches, mosques and other structures (all Frankish and Turkish structures were removed after independence).

In 1687 the Venetians opened fire on the ruling Turks on the Acropolis causing a massive explosion (the Ottomans stored gunpowder in the Parthenon) that severely damaged the buildings.

Entry to the Acropolis is through the **Beulé Gate**, built in the 3rd century AD.

Beyond it is the **Propylaia**, built 437–432 BC, which formed the monumental entrance to the Acropolis. The western portico has six imposing double-columns (Doric on the outside and Ionic inside) and the ceiling was painted dark blue with gold stars. One of the Propylaia's five gates led to the **Panathenaic Way**, the route taken by the Panathenaic procession at the festival dedicated to Athena.

The elegant, small **Temple of Athena Nike** (5, B5), originally built by Callicrates (c 420 BC) on the southwestern edge, has undergone several reconstructions and was removed altogether in late 2002 to be repaired off-site and then reconstructed (it had yet to reappear in 2006). Only fragments remain of the frieze that depicted victory scenes from battles.

WORK IN PROGRESS

Since 1975 scores of archaeologists, engineers and stonemasons have been working on the Acropolis conservation effort, with cranes and scaffolding virtually a permanent fixture. The massive undertaking to redress damage done by previous botched restorations using iron clamps that rusted, and deterioration from age, wear and tear and acid rain is expected to continue for some years and to the tune of millions of euros. Many temples have been completely disassembled and rebuilt on site, as have some of the Parthenon's columns.

A statue of Athena that once graced the temple was most likely destroyed by the Persians.

The **Erechtheion** was built on the Acropolis' most sacred spot, where, in a contest for the city, Poseidon struck the ground with his trident producing a spring of water and Athena in turn produced the olive tree (she won).

Named after Erichthonius, the mythical king of Athens, the temple was completed in 420 BC and housed the cults of Athena, Poseidon and Erichthonius. The six column maidens are the famous **Caryatids**, modelled on the women from Karyai. The ones you see are plaster casts. The originals (except for one taken by Lord Elgin, which is now in London's British Museum) are in the Acropolis Museum.

The symbol of the glory of ancient Greece, the **Parthenon** (Virgin's Chamber) stands on the highest point of the Acropolis. It is the largest Doric temple ever completed in Greece and the only one built entirely of Pentelic marble. It was the centrepiece of Pericles' Acropolis, finished in time for the Great Panathenaic Festival of 438 BC. As well as housing the great statue of Athena, by Pheidias, the Parthenon served as the treasury for the Delian League. The temple had eight fluted Doric columns at either end and 17 on each side ingeniously curved to create an optical illusion of a harmonious, perfect form. Brightly coloured and gilded sculptured friezes ran all the way around (159.5m long) depicting the various battles of the times and the Panathenaic procession. Most of the friezes were damaged in the 1687 explosion, but the greatest existing sections (more than 75m) are in the British Museum.

Reserved strictly for privileged initiates, the holy *cella* (inner room) contained the colossal 10m-high gold and ivory statue of Athena Parthenos, one of the wonders of the ancient world. The tyrant Lachares is said to have stripped the gold from the statue to pay his troops.

Remnants of a rich and glorious past, viewed from Filopappou Hill

ACROPOLIS MUSEUM (5, C6)

At the time of writing, Athens' long-awaited, new Acropolis Museum was to open in stages in 2007, at the southern foot of the Acropolis. The priceless sculptures and reliefs from the site, long held in the old museum on the Acropolis, were to be slowly transferred to their new €130 million home in a gradual and grand public spectacle.

INFORMATION

- ☎ 210 321 0219
- 💻 www.culture.gr
- ✉ cnr Dionysiou Areopagitou & Makrigianni (new museum)
- € old museum admission included in the €12 Acropolis entry; no costs available for the new museum at the time of writing
- ⏱ 8am-7.30pm (8am-5pm Nov-Mar)
- ℹ new museum opening in stages from 2007; entry from Dionysiou Areopagitou
- Ⓜ Akropoli
- ♿ good for old museum; excellent for new museum
- ✕ from 2007 at the new museum

Prized exhibits include four of the five surviving **Caryatids** (the fifth is in the British Museum) and the large collection of **6th-century BC Korai** (maiden) statues uncovered from a pit on the Acropolis, where the Athenians buried them after the Battle of Salamis. Each one holds an offering to the goddess Athena.

The new museum will exhibit thousands of artefacts never before seen by the public, with the massive exhibition space accommodating 10 times the number of pieces on display at the old museum, most of which had been in storage. The museum also hopes to eventually consolidate all the surviving treasures of the Acropolis held in other museums in Greece and abroad. The top-floor glass atrium gallery will showcase the Parthenon's sculptures, metopes and the frieze, including the section depicting the Olympians at the Panathenaic procession. Spaces for the missing pieces – about half the frieze is in the British Museum – will pose an open invitation for their return.

Excavation works uncovered the remains of an Athenian city dating back to prehistoric times. More than 2000 sq metres of the old city can be seen through a series of ramps and glass floors.

LOST YOUR MARBLES?

The Parthenon marbles were hacked off the temple in 1801 by the British Ambassador in Constantinople, Lord Elgin, who sold them to the British Museum, which in turn scrubbed them in the false belief that they should be white, when in fact they were colourfully painted. The museum has rejected continuous campaigns for their return.

PLAKA (MAP 11)

Plaka, the historic neighbourhood located below the Acropolis, is a magnet for tourists and Athenians alike – a colourful and lively mix of old Athens with today's busy restaurants, cafés, tourist shops and galleries. Beyond the busy tourist drag, exploring Plaka's stone-paved narrow streets is a rewarding journey, with many significant monuments and ancient, Byzantine and Ottoman structures providing a palpable sense of history. Streets such as Adrianou and Tripodon follow the paths of ancient roads.

INFORMATION

€ free

Ⓜ Syntagma, Akropoli, Monastiraki

✕ Klepsidra (Thrasyvoulou 9), Amalthia Cafe (Tripodon 16)

One of Plaka's pleasant surprises is the **Anafiotika** quarter, a picturesque labyrinth of quiet, narrow, winding paths with island-style houses decorated with bougainvillea and bright pots of colour.

The whitewashed Cycladic-style houses were built by homesick stonemasons from the island of Anafi, brought in to build the king's palace during the rebuilding of Athens after independence. It is still home to many of their descendants. The 17th-century **Church of Agios Georgios** (St George of the Rock; 11, B3) marks the entrance to Anafiotika, with the 1847 **Church of Agios Simeon** (11, A3) to the northwest.

FOUNDATION STONES

Many of the small Byzantine churches in Plaka were built on the site of ancient temples in an attempt to crush the pagan elements – some have visible segments of temples used in the new structure. Most of the churches in Plaka still operate today, and the traditional Easter services attract people from all over Athens.

Many neoclassical buildings in Plaka have been meticulously restored, as gentrification has made Plaka one of Athens' more exclusive neighbourhoods. The neoclassical **Old Athens University** (11, A2) building on the corner of Theorias and Klepsidras is now a museum. Many Plaka streets are pedestrian-only, adding to the area's charm.

The 17th-century Church of Agios Georgios, stark white against an azure sky

NATIONAL ARCHAEOLOGICAL MUSEUM (4, C2)

Greece's pre-eminent museum houses the world's largest and finest collection of Greek antiquities.

The museum's treasures date back to the Neolithic era (6800 BC) and include antiquities from the Bronze Age, Cycladic, Minoan, Mycenaean and classical periods, with exquisite pottery and frescoes, jewellery and countless other objects from throughout Greece.

Following a major refurbishment, the museum has its collection beautifully presented, with hundreds of pieces held in storage for years now on display.

Some of the most important exhibits are grouped on the 1st floor in the prehistoric collection, including the fabulous collection of **Mycenaean antiquities** in Gallery 4 (see below).

The **Cycladic collection**, which is located in Gallery 6, includes the superb figurines of the 3rd and 2nd century BC that inspired artists such as Picasso.

Some of the highlights of the Sculpture collection include the colossal 3m marble 600 BC **Sounion Kouros** (Gallery 8) found at the Temple of Poseidon, the 460 BC bronze **statue of Zeus or Poseidon** (no one really knows which god) holding a thunderbolt or trident (Gallery 15) and the striking 2nd-century-BC statue of a **horse and young rider** (Gallery 21), recovered from a shipwreck.

Another big crowd-puller is the Thira gallery, with the spectacular **Minoan frescos** from Santorini.

The superb **pottery collection** traces the development of pottery from the Bronze Age, including the famous Attic black-figured pottery and the uniquely Athenian slender Attic white Lekythoi vases depicting scenes at tombs.

At the time of writing the final two galleries housing the rich Egyptian collection and the Stathatos collection were set to reopen in 2007.

INFORMATION

☎ 210 821 7717
🖳 www.culture.gr
✉ 28 Oktovriou-Patission 44, Athens
€ €7/3
🕙 8am-7pm Tue-Sun (1-7pm Mon, 8am-5pm Tue-Sun Nov-Mar)
Ⓜ Viktoria
🚌 2, 4, 5, 9 or 11
♿ excellent

AGAMEMNON'S DEATH MASK

One of the most significant exhibits is the exquisite Mycenaean gold collection, found in unlooted tombs excavated by Heinrich Schliemann at Mycenae from 1847 to 1876. The finds correspond with Homer's famous tale in the *Iliad* and *Odyssey*. Despite modern dating techniques suggesting it belonged to an earlier king, the 1600 BC gold funerary mask is believed to be Agamemnon's.

ANCIENT PROMENADE (4, B6)

Once choked by traffic and pollution, the streets around Athens' historic centre have been transformed into a spectacular 3km pedestrian promenade connecting the city's most significant ancient sites.

This new 'open museum', reputedly Europe's longest pedestrian precinct, is a quiet and green traffic-free oasis showcasing the beauty of the old city and incorporating it into the modern life of the city.

In the evening, locals and tourists alike delight in a leisurely *volta* (stroll) along the wide cobblestone promenade, which winds its way around the foothills of the floodlit Acropolis. All key monuments and temples along the route have been brilliantly illuminated by French designer Pierre Bideau.

The promenade starts in the south at Dionysiou Areopagitou, opposite the Temple of Olympian Zeus, and continues along the southern foothills of the Acropolis, past the Odeon of Herodes Atticus, to the foot of Filopappou Hill. The pedestrian zone continues along Apostolou Pavlou past the open-air cinema, Thisseion (p94), and rows of busy cafés all the way to the Ancient Agora. It then branches off west from Thisio to Keramikos all the way to Gazi, and north along Adrianou to Monastiraki, where the pedestrian zone continues to the Roman Agora towards the atmospheric streets of Plaka.

INFORMATION

✉ Thisio-Akropoli
€ free
Ⓜ Monastiraki, Thisio, Akropoli

The promenade is the most significant development in the historic centre since the award-winning paths and landscaping around the Acropolis and Filopappou Hill were completed in 1957 by acclaimed architect and philosopher Dimitris Pikionis.

Open-air sculpture exhibitions, book fairs and buskers add to the festive atmosphere in the evenings, while the busy cafés make Thisio one of the city's liveliest precincts.

CITY FACELIFT

The pedestrian promenade is part of the ambitious Unification of Archaeological Sites' masterplan for the city. Apart from the continuing pedestrianisation programme, efforts to improve the aesthetics and quality of life of the city involved the restoration of key monuments around Athens, the removal of hundreds of ugly billboards, creation of green spaces, restoration of neoclassical mansions, and painting the façades of thousands of buildings.

SYNTAGMA & THE PARLIAMENT (5, E4)

Busy Syntagma Sq (Plateia Syntagmatos; Constitution Sq) is crowned by the grand Parliament, originally built as a palace for King Otto, the Bavarian prince installed by the allies after Greek independence. It remained a royal palace until 1935, when it became the seat of the Greek Parliament. Its colourful history includes a stint as a shelter for homeless refugees from Asia Minor.

Only the library, which often hosts exhibits, is open to the public.

In the Parliament forecourt, the **Tomb of the Unknown Soldier**, a monument to the country's fallen, is guarded by the striking *evzones* (presidential guards) in traditional uniform. The sculpture of a dying soldier makes a stunning backdrop for the popular changing of the guard ceremony (see below).

INFORMATION

- 🖳 www.culture.gr
- ✉ Syntagma Sq, Syntagma
- € free
- 🕑 Parliament library 9am-1.30pm Mon-Fri
- Ⓜ Syntagma
- ♿ good

The grand square, laid out in 1835 by designers of the new capital, has undergone several face-lifts and remains the centre point of the city, with the cafés and central fountain being a popular meeting point.

The historic Grand Bretagne (p98), one of the remaining original buildings, was built in 1862 to accommodate visiting dignitaries, a role it maintains today. The Nazis made it their headquarters during WWII and it was the site of an attempt to blow up Winston Churchill on Christmas Eve 1944. The refurbishment of the King George II palace (p98), next door to the Grand Bretagne, and other grand buildings around the square has gone some way to counterbalancing the tacky McDonald's and fast-food joints that line the other side.

POM-POM PARADE

Parliament is guarded day and night by *evzones,* the presidential guards in traditional uniforms of short kilts and pom-pom shoes, who stand rigid and stony faced during their shifts. On the hour, every hour, three replacements march up Vas Sofias and arrive for a colourful changing of the guard ceremony. On Sunday and on major holidays, the 6ft-plus *evzones* come out in the full regalia for an extended affair with military band (10.45am). The ceremonial costume is based on that worn by *klephts,* the rebels of the War of Independence – the red fez symbolises bloodshed and the white kilts have 400 pleats, one for every year of Turkish occupation. *Evzones* groupies can see more changing of the guard routines behind the gardens at the **presidential palace** (5, F5; Irodou Attikou).

ANCIENT AGORA (5, A4)

The best-preserved *agora* (market or place of assembly) in Greece gives invaluable insight into the workings of ancient Athens. The Agora was the centre of civic life and government, a bustling hub of social activity, housing the law courts and the market. Socrates came here to expound his philosophy, and in AD 49 St Paul came to win converts to Christianity.

First developed in the 6th century BC, the Agora was destroyed by the Persians in 480 BC, then rebuilt and flourished until AD 267 when the Heruli, a Gothic tribe from Scandinavia, destroyed it.

There is a useful model of this huge site in the **Agora Museum** in the restored 138 BC **Stoa of Attalos**, which has a significant collection of finds, including a 5th-century terracotta water clock used to time speeches. The 45-column, two-storey stoa was essentially an elite shopping arcade and hang-out for rich Athenians; they came here to watch the Panathenaic procession.

During Byzantine, Frankish and Ottoman eras, the area was

INFORMATION

- ☎ 210 321 0185
- 🖳 www.culture.gr
- ✉ Adrianou 24, Monastiraki
- € €4 (or free with Acropolis pass)
- 🕗 8am-7.30pm (11am-7.30pm Mon, 8am-5pm Nov-Mar)
- ℹ Entrances on Adrianou, Thisiou & Vrysakiou
- Ⓜ Monastiraki, Thisio

Take a walk back in time at Agora Museum

covered in houses. More than 400 modern buildings were demolished to uncover the Agora when the site was excavated and the Stoa of Attalos reconstructed in 1953–56. The 11th-century **Church of the Holy Apostles of Solakis** (p34) is the only remaining Byzantine structure.

The **Temple of Hephaestus**, also known as the Thisseion on the western end, was dedicated to the god of metallurgy and was surrounded by foundries and metal workshops. Built in 449 BC, it is the best-preserved Doric temple in Greece, with 36 columns and a frieze on the eastern side depicting nine of the 12 labours of Heracles.

The site has many significant ruins and building foundations, including statues from the Odeon of Agrippa; the Stoas of Zeus Eleftherios (Freedom), Basileios (Royalty) and Poikile (Painted Stoa); the Metroon (Record Office); the prison; and the Tholos (where civic dinners were held).

DON'T MISS

- Great drain and *in situ* inscribed boundary stone ('I am the boundary of the Agora')
- Fine Byzantine frescoes in the Church of the Holy Apostles of Solakis
- Headless statue of Roman emperor Hadrian

ROMAN ATHENS (11, A2)

Under Roman rule, the city's civic centre was moved to the **Roman Agora**. The partly excavated site features the foundations of several structures, including a 1st-century, 68-seat public latrine to the right of the entry, and a *propylon* (entrance) at the southeastern corner.

While some shops have been excavated, the main surviving feature is the well-preserved **Gate of Athena Archegetis**, flanked by four Doric columns, which was erected in the 1st century AD and financed by Julius Caesar.

The innovative Tower of the Winds

The octagonal **Tower of the Winds**, next to the Agora, is thought to predate the Agora, built about 150–125 BC by the astronomer Andronicus. It is considered an ingenious construction, functioning as a sundial, weather vane, water clock and compass. Made of Pentelic marble, it had a bronze triton as a weather vane and reliefs of eight wind figures on each side depicting the wind patterns.

The Tower of the Winds was converted to a church and then used for dervishes under Ottoman rule. The **Fethiye Djami mosque** on the northern side of the Agora is one of the city's few surviving reminders of Ottoman times.

Closer to Monastiraki station is the surviving part of the **Hadrian's Library** (5, A1), once the most luxurious public building in the city. Erected around AD 132, it had an internal courtyard and pool and was bordered by 100 columns. It was destroyed in AD 267 during the Herulian invasion. The remains of **Megali Panagia**, believed to be the oldest Christian Church in Athens, can be seen in the garden of Hadrian's Library, including parts of the mosaic floor. During the Ottoman period it was a bazaar.

ROMAN BATHS

Excavations for a ventilation shaft for the metro revealed the well-preserved ruins of a large Roman bath complex near Syntagma. The Roman Baths (5, D5), which extend into the National Gardens, were established near the Ilissos River after the Herulian raids in the 3rd century AD; they were destroyed and repaired again in the 5th or 6th century.

BENAKI MUSEUM (5, F4)

Housed in the stunning former home of the Benaki family, this is the oldest private museum in Greece and ranks among its best. It was founded in 1930 by Antonis Benakis, son of the wealthy Alexandrian merchant Emmanuel Benakis.

The collection represents the historical and cultural development of Greece and Hellenism. It includes Benakis' eclectic acquisitions from Asia and Europe and pieces from the Byzantine and post-Byzantine eras. The museum has received many significant collections and major donations since it was inaugurated in 1931.

A 10-year US$20-million renovation completed in 2000 refurbished all the galleries. More than 20,000 items are on display chronologically over four levels, beginning with prehistory and continuing on to the formation of the modern Greek state. It has an excellent **Byzantine collection** and a gallery focusing on the development of Hellenism during foreign domination.

The spectrum of Greek cultural history is covered, including Karaghiozi shadow puppets, a stunning array of costumes, jewellery and textiles, and paintings that include early works by El Greco (Domenicos Theotokopoulos).

The antiquities collection includes Bronze Age finds from Mycenae and Thessaly and Cycladic pottery, while the Egyptian collection includes Greco-Roman Fayum funerary portraits.

Benakis' heart is immured inside the museum's entrance, but the soul of Greece is well enshrined in his gift to the country.

There is a fine restaurant on the terrace overlooking the National Gardens and an excellent gift shop. The Benaki also has an impressive Benaki Museum Pireos Annexe (p29) and a dedicated Islamic Art Museum (p30) housing its extensive collection.

INFORMATION

- ☎ 210 367 1000
- 🖥 www.benaki.gr
- ✉ Koumbari 1 (cnr Koumbari & Vas Sofias), Kolonaki
- € permanent collection & temporary exhibitions €6, temporary exhibitions €3, admission free Thu
- 🕑 9am-5pm Mon, Wed, Fri & Sat, 9am-midnight Thu, 9am-3pm Sun
- Ⓜ Syntagma
- ♿ good
- ✗ Kylikeion

Money really does talk; a gold medallion

DON'T MISS

- Euboia treasure with 3000 BC gold and silver cups
- Mycenaean gold jewellery from Thebes
- Two signed El Greco paintings
- Two mid-18th-century wood-carved reception rooms from Kozani mansions

LYKAVITTOS HILL (6, A1)

Rising starkly from the sea of apartments blocks below, Lykavittos is the other hill that dominates central Athens, along with the Acropolis. The name means 'Hill of Wolves' but these days there is barely a dog on the rocky crag, which rises 272.7m.

INFORMATION

- ☎ 210 722 7092
- ✉ funicular at cnr Aristippou & Ploutarhou, Lykavittos
- € free
- ⓨ 9am-11.45pm, runs every 30min
- Ⓜ Evangelismos, then funicular (return €4)
- ⓧ Orizontes (p74)

If you are not game to take the steep walk, a funicular railway takes you through a tunnel to the peak of Lykavittos. At night the view is spectacular and the air is cool, but even during the day this is a great place to get some perspective on the Athens panorama. On a clear day you can see the island of Aegina and the Peloponnese from the top.

On the summit, the white **Chapel of Agios Georgios**, impressively floodlit at night, stands on the site of an ancient temple that was once dedicated to Zeus. There are two cannons just below on the western side that fire salutes on special occasions. Regular church services are held at the chapel, the most important being on 23 April, the day of the patron saint, St George, and Good Friday, when there is a moving candlelight procession along the hill.

There are walking paths through the cypress- and pine-covered hill. The open-air Lykavittos Theatre, built in 1964 on a former quarry site on the northern slope, hosts concerts and theatrical performances in summer.

The Orizontes restaurant and café at the top of the hill has superb views.

OPEN-AIR CONCERTS

In summer, the **Lykavittos Theatre** (6, A1) hosts evening concerts and theatre. The open-air amphitheatre is one of the cooler (literally) venues in town, with sensational views from the top rows. The surrounding rock face is often dotted with precariously perched people getting a free show. For information contact the **Hellenic Festival box office** (☎ 210 322 1459; www .hellenicfestival.gr; Panepistimiou 39).

MUSEUM OF CYCLADIC & ANCIENT GREEK ART (5, F4)

This exceptional private museum houses the biggest independent collection of Cycladic art in the world, as well as an impressive collection of ancient Greek art. The museum was custom-built in 1986 for the personal collection of Nicholas and Dolly Goulandris, members of one of Greece's richest shipping families. It has since enriched its collection and expanded to the stunning 19th-century Stathatos mansion, designed by Ernst Ziller, and an adjacent wing used for temporary exhibitions.

The museum's collection is well presented, largely chronologically, on four floors. Although it comprises pieces dated to AD 400, the emphasis is on the Cycladic civilisation that flourished in the Aegean around the sacred island of Delos from 3200 to 2000 BC.

INFORMATION
- ☎ 210 722 8321
- 🖥 www.cycladic.gr
- ✉ Neofytou Douka 4 (cnr Vas Sofias & Irodotou), Kolonaki
- € €5
- 🕙 10am-4pm Mon, Thu & Fri, 10am-8pm Wed (summer), 10am-3pm Sat
- Ⓜ Evangelismos
- ♿ only from Neofytou Douka entrance
- ✗ on-site café

DON'T MISS
- Cycladic '*Modigliani*' c 2800-2300 BC (1st fl, case 1)
- *Drinker* c 2800-2300 BC (1st fl, case 17)
- 5th-century BC water jug (2nd fl, case 24)
- *Athenians at the Symposion* (2nd fl, case 32)

The Cycladic collection, displayed on the 1st floor, includes life-sized marble statues, tiny figurines and pottery from the period. The distinctive, white, minimalist slender figurines of the Cycladic era, depicting raw human forms, have long inspired modern artists and sculptors, including Picasso, Modigliani and Henry Moore.

On the 4th floor, the Karolos Politis collection has pieces from the Mycenaean period to the 14th century, including 8th-century-BC Corinthian bronze helmets and fine terracotta vases.

The 2nd floor presents Greek artefacts from the Bronze Age (2nd millennium BC) through to the Late Roman period (4th century AD).

The Thanos Zintilis collection of Cypriot antiquities on the 3rd floor is the largest Cypriot collection in Greece.

The pleasant atrium café is a great pit stop and the gift shop is well worth a look.

NATIONAL ART GALLERY (6, B3)

Greece's premiere art gallery showcases its permanent collection of modern Greek art and hosts major international exhibitions.

The gallery celebrated its centenary in 2000 by inaugurating its €3.4-million face-lift and extension. Exhibition space was added (2000 sq metres) and the latest technology installed, including an audio system with CD tours in English and Greek.

The history of Greek art is presented in chronological lines and themes exploring the country's unique art movements; some of the best examples of Greek art are shown. Prize exhibits include three **masterpieces from El Greco**, including *The Burial of Christ*, acquired for US$700,000 in 2000, and *St Peter*.

INFORMATION

☎ 210 723 5937
🖳 www.culture.gr
✉ Vas Konstantinou 50, Athens
€ €6.50
🕙 9am-3pm & 6-9pm Mon & Wed,
9am-3pm Thu-Sat, 10am-2pm Sun
Ⓜ Evangelismos
♿ good
🍴 Flocafé

The art exhibition begins with a small post-Byzantine collection, followed by the Eptanesian School of artists, originally from the Ionian islands, who led the transition from Byzantine to secular painting. Among the most significant pieces are portraits and historical scenes from the War of Independence and the early years of the Greek state.

The 2nd floor presents 20th-century painters, including the early artists Parthenis and Maleas and the work of renowned 1930s-generation artists such as Tsarouchis and Hadjikyriakos-Ghikas. Postwar artists get less wall space; this should change in further planned expansions.

The gallery's sculpture collection is now housed at the National Glyptoteque (p37) in Goudi.

DON'T MISS

- Vrysakis' *Exodus from Messolongi*
- Gyzis' *Behold the Celestial Bridegroom Cometh*
- surrealist Engonopoulos' *Delos*
- Lytras' *The Kiss*
- El Greco's *Concert of Angels*

The art begins outside the National Art Gallery

FILOPAPPOU HILL & HILL OF THE PNYX (5, A5)

Also known as the Hill of the Muses, pine- and cypress-clad Filopappou Hill, southwest of the Acropolis, is a pleasant place for a wander, offering great views of the Acropolis and beyond, to the plains of Attica and the Saronic Gulf.

The **Monument of Filopappos** stands on the summit, built in AD 114–16 in honour of prominent Roman governor Julius Antiochus Filopappos, who is depicted in a frieze driving his chariot.

A fort to defend Athens was built here earlier in 294 BC.

A paved road next to Dionysos taverna, on Dionysiou Areopagitou, leads you to the 16th-century **Church of Agios Dimitrios Loumbardiaris** (from the Greek word for cannon), named after an incident in which a Turkish garrison on the Acropolis allegedly tried to fire a cannon on Christians gathered at the church, but the gunners were killed by a miraculous thunderbolt.

Sensitively restored in the 1950s, the church has some fine frescoes and is popular for baptisms and weddings (the adjacent café is a cool retreat with great views). On the first day of Lent, 'Clean Monday', Filopappos is invaded by people picnicking and flying kites, as is customary throughout Athens.

To the north of Filopappou Hill is the smaller **Hill of the Pnyx**. This was the meeting place of the Democratic Assembly in the 5th century BC. Aristides, Demosthenes, Pericles and Themistocles were among the great orators who addressed assemblies here.

INFORMATION

✉ Filopappou Hill, off Dionysiou Areopagitou
€ free
Ⓜ Akropoli
✕ on-site café

Monument of Filopappos

Northwest of Filopappou you'll find the **Hill of the Nymphs**, with the 1840s **Old Athens Observatory** (4, A6) on the summit.

Below the observatory is the **Church of Agia Marina** (7, C3), which has a lively annual festival on 17 July, celebrated with a colourful street fair. Filopappou has many other smaller paths for walks and is popular with joggers, but caution should be exercised at night.

HILL OF DANCE

Since 1965, the open-air theatre on Filopappou Hill has been the venue for lively performances of traditional Greek folk music and dance by the renowned Dora Stratou Dance Theatre (see p82). The theatre is considered a living folk museum, with dancers performing hundreds of different dances from around Greece in authentic costumes that are part of the group's extensive museum collection.

BYZANTINE & CHRISTIAN MUSEUM (6, A3)

The Byzantine and Christian Museum is one of the city's pre-eminent galleries. Its priceless collection of early Christian and Byzantine art showcases the glory of Byzantium, which is slowly claiming its rightful place as a significant epoch in history after long being overshadowed by ancient Greece.

Housed on the pretty grounds of the former Villa Ilissia, the museum is a welcome break from the city hubbub.

INFORMATION

- ☎ 210 723 2178
- 🖳 www.culture.gr
- ✉ Vas Sofias 22, Athens
- € €4, extra charge for special temporary exhibitions, admission free for the mobility impaired
- 🕙 8.30am-6pm Tue-Sun
- ⓘ hosts Byzantine & classical concerts in summer
- Ⓜ Evangelismos
- ♿ excellent
- ✗ on-site restaurant & café planned

Christian art, dating from the 4th to 15th century, that sheds light on Byzantine and post-Byzantine culture is beautifully presented with themed displays in a multi-level underground gallery.

Visitors can see exquisite icons, early Christian sculptures, frescoes, ceramics, wall paintings, Coptic embroideries, coins, jewellery and parchment manuscripts. The precious collection of gold and silver ecclesiastical vestments and secular items include the **Mytiline treasure**.

Other highlights of the museum are the **Christian reliefs** from the Parthenon and Christian temples on the Acropolis and the 13th-century **church-dome fresco**.

At the time of research a new wing presenting the post-Byzantine collection up to the 19th century was due to open in 2007. It will bring to light a greater selection of the museum's collection of more than 15,000 artefacts from Greece and other reaches of the Byzantine empire.

The elegant Tuscan-style villa of the Duchess de Plaisance that previously housed the museum will be used for temporary exhibitions, a café and gift shop. The existing gift shop has some fine icons.

DON'T MISS

- mosaic icon of the Virgin, the *Episkepsis*
- double-sided, 13th-century icon with St George on the front
- 4th-century sculpture of Orpheus playing the lyre, surrounded by animals

TEMPLE OF OLYMPIAN ZEUS (5, D6)

The colossal Temple of Olympian Zeus (or Olympeion) is the largest in Greece and took more than 700 years to build. The 104 Corinthian columns stood 17m high with a base diameter of 1.7m. Fifteen remain today – one lies on the ground having fallen in a gale in 1852.

Foundations of a small temple dedicated to the cult of Olympian Zeus (dated 590–560 BC) lie on the site. Peisistratos began building a temple twice its size in the 6th century BC on the western bank of the Ilissos River, but it was abandoned due to a lack of funds.

A succession of leaders tried to finish the temple, making adjustments to the original plans along the way, which explains inconsistencies in the temple. Hadrian finally took credit for finishing the task in AD 131. The temple had a giant gold and ivory statue of Zeus and one of Hadrian.

Hadrian's Arch once linked a thoroughfare heading past the Lysicrates Monument (see below) along the **Street of Tripods**, where 'tripod' trophies were dedicated to Dionysos by winners of ancient drama contests. Made of Pentelic marble, the decorative Roman-style arch was erected in Hadrian's honour in AD 132, after the consecration of the temple, for which it was a kind of architectural preface. It was also intended as a city gate marking the border of the ancient and new Roman cities. The inscription on the northwestern frieze reads 'This is Athens, the ancient city of Theseus'. On the other side, it says 'This is the city of Hadrian, and not of Theseus'. There was probably a statue of Theseus or Hadrian on each side.

INFORMATION

☎ 210 922 6330
🖳 www.culture.gr
✉ Vas Olgas, Athens
€ €2 (free with Acropolis pass)
🕓 8am-7.30pm (8am-5pm Nov-Mar)
Ⓜ Akropoli

LYSICRATES MONUMENT

The 335–334 BC monument (11, B3) was erected by Lysicrates, a choragus (sponsor) of the drama contests, to display the bronze tripod trophies. The circular building, with six Corinthian columns and a frieze showing scenes from Dionysos' life, is the only choragic monument preserved almost complete.

In 1669 it was incorporated into a Capucin monastery and used as a library, in which Lord Byron allegedly wrote part of *Childe Harold*.

ANCIENT THEATRES (5, C5)

The **Theatre of Dionysos** (5, C5), on the Acropolis' southeastern slope, was built on the site of the Dionysia Festival, during which there were contests, men clad in goatskins sang and danced, and the masses feasted and partied.

The first theatre, built in the 6th century BC, was made of timber. During the golden age, politicians sponsored productions of the dramas and comedies of Aeschylus, Sophocles, Euripides and Aristophanes. Reconstructed in stone and marble by Lykourgos between 342 and 326 BC, the theatre had seating for more than 15,000 spectators, with 64 tiers of seats. Only about 20 survive. An altar to Dionysos once stood in the middle of the orchestra pit. The marble thrones on the lower levels were reserved for dignitaries and priests – the grand one in the centre was for the priest of Dionysos. It is identifiable today by the lions' paws, satyrs and griffins carved on the back. The plebs had to make do with the limestone seating.

INFORMATION

- ☎ 210 322 4625
- 🖳 www.culture.gr
- ✉ Dionysiou Areopagitou, Makrigianni
- € €2 (free with Acropolis pass)
- ☾ 8am-7.30pm (8am-5pm Nov-Mar)
- Ⓜ Akropoli

DON'T MISS

- 2nd-century-BC relief of Dionysos' exploits (backstage)
- the *Asclepion* sanctuary above the Stoa of Eumenes
- a show at the Odeon of Herodes Atticus

The **Odeon of Herodes Atticus** (5, B5) was built in AD 161 in memory of his wife, Regilla, and was one of ancient Athens' last grand public buildings. The semicircular theatre had a cedar roof over parts of the stage and an imposing three-storey stage building of arches.

Excavated in the 1850s, the theatre was restored in time for the 1955 Hellenic Festival and remains Athens' premiere, and most inspiring, venue for summer performances of drama, music and dance. It is only open during performances but can be viewed from the Acropolis above.

Between the two theatres is the **Stoa of Eumenes** (5, B5), an arched portico designed as a promenade to protect theatre patrons from the sun.

Hope you don't suffer from vertigo – a bird's-eye view of the Theatre of Dionysos

KERAMIKOS (7, C2)

As well as being the largest and best-preserved classical necropolis, the Keramikos cemetery is a little oasis in downtown Athens. It is now accessed by the pedestrian promenade linking the key archaeological sites.

Keramikos is also the site of the once-massive **Dipylon Gate**, where in antiquity the processions entered the city on their way to the Acropolis via the Ancient Agora. These days you have to search for the plaque that marks the ruins of the gate, but it all starts to make sense as you see the Acropolis ahead.

You can also see the site of the **Sacred Gate** through which pilgrims entered to travel along the Sacred Way to Eleusis.

Named after the potter's workshops that once thrived in the area, the cemetery was the burial ground for Athenians from 3000 BC to the 6th century AD. The grand **Street of Tombs**, where elite Athenians were buried, has some impressive tombs, notably the 4th-century-BC marble bull in the plot of Dionysos of Kollytos. The one *in situ* is a replica – the original and many other precious finds, including pottery, funerary offerings, toys and even knucklebones sets, are in the excellent, small **Oberlaender Museum** on the site.

Less visited than many other sites, Keramikos is green and peaceful and a delight in spring when the wildflowers are in bloom. Turtles crawl about, while frogs inhabit the spring that runs through the site.

Excavation work for an aborted metro station originally planned next to the site uncovered a wealth of treasures, including more than 7000 *ostraka* (shards of pottery marked with the names of ostracised Athenian statesmen).

INFORMATION

☎ 210 346 3552
🖳 www.culture.gr
✉ Ermou 148, Thisio
€ €2 (free with Acropolis pass)
🕑 8am-7.30pm (11am-7.30pm Mon, 8am-5pm Nov-Mar)
Ⓜ Thisio

THEMISTOCLEAN WALL

In the Keramikos site you can see the longest and best preserved section of the 479 BC Themistoclean wall, a 6.5km wall built around Athens to protect the city. The wall was reinforced with towers and had 15 gates leading to other parts of Attica and Piraeus. You can see a part of the wall under the Islamic Art Museum (p30) and various parts of the city, while the remains of one of the gates is on display opposite and underneath the National Bank of Greece building on Eolou.

ATHENS BY THE SEA (1, B3)

Most visitors exploring Athens seem to forget the Greek capital is a coastal city. Despite notoriously hot summers, heading to the beach was never part of the average tourist's itinerary. However, ongoing waterfront redevelopment, new green zones and the new tram line along the coast have helped open up the sea to the city.

INFORMATION

- Ⓜ Faliro
- € free
- 🚊 Line 4 (Faliro), Line 5 (Glyfada)
- 🚌 A2, E22 from Panepistimiou

The coastline stretches about 25km from Faliro to Glyfada and all the way to the southern-most suburb of Vouliagmeni. It's a pleasant, if patchy, part of the city where Athenians flock to the beaches, promenade on summer evenings and party at the beach nightclubs.

A scenic tram line from Syntagma runs south along Posidonos avenue to Glyfada, while a second route heads north along the coast to Alimo, Palio Faliro and the sports stadiums near Piraeus.

Along the way you will find restaurants, bars and cafés, children's playgrounds, a go-cart track, marinas, an open-air cinema and luna park, as well as former Olympics venues, some of which are used for concerts and cultural events.

Following the clean up of the Saronic Gulf and coastal waters of Athens, swimming at the sandy beaches is no longer the risky business it was a decade ago. Some Athens beaches even have Blue Flag status (the European clean beach rating system). The crowds are the main drawback.

A 50m footbridge leads directly from the old racecourse on Syngrou to the redeveloped Faliron Delta coastal zone; it is planned this will eventually become a waterfront leisure and entertainment precinct.

Glyfada's busy shopping strip has all the top-name stores, while Glyfada beach boasts cafés, fish taverns and restaurants, the classiest organised beach, chic beach bars and summer nightclubs.

BEACH BABIES

Athenians have always flocked to the sea in summer. While there are free public beaches along the coast, the Greeks are not keen on roughing it – thus the institution of organised beach resorts with admission charges. These, mostly privatised, beaches have sun beds, cafés and bars, and lockers and showers, while the fancier ones have playgrounds, beach-volleyball facilities, water sports and even cabanas (p117).

Sights & Activities

MUSEUMS

See also Highlights (p10) and art museums (p36).

Benaki Museum Pireos Annexe (7, A3)

This massive new annexe of the Benaki museum is in a former industrial building on busy Pireos St. It hosts regular visual arts, cultural and historical exhibitions as well as major international shows. There's a café and excellent gift store.

☎ 210 345 3111 🖥 www .benaki.gr ✉ Pireos 138 (cnr Andronikou), Gazi € per exhibition €2 ⏰ 10am-6pm Wed & Thu-Sun, 10am-10pm Fri & Sat 🚌 811 🚋 21

Centre of Folk Art & Tradition (11, C2)

The rooms in the mansion of famous folklorist Angeliki Hatzimichalis, built in the 1920s, have been set up to depict the traditional pastoral Greek way of life, including an old kitchen and its stove and utensils and ceramic plates from Skyros. There's also a chapel, regional costumes, embroideries, weaving machines, ceramic vases and family portraits. At the

time of writing, it was being refurbished.

☎ 210 324 3972 ✉ Hatzimihali Agelikis 6, Plaka € free ⏰ 9am-1pm & 5-9pm Tue-Fri, 9am-1pm Sat & Sun Ⓜ Akropoli, Syntagma

City of Athens Museum (5, D3)

Once the residence of King Otto and Queen Amalia (while the royal palace was being built), the museum contains some of the royal

couple's personal items and furniture – including the throne. Covering the history of Athens from the end of the Middle Ages to today, the rich displays include paintings by leading Greek and foreign artists, and models of 19th-century Athens.

☎ 210 324 6164 🖥 www .athenscitymuseum.gr ✉ Paparigopoulou 5 & 7, Panepistimio € €3 ⏰ 9am-4pm Mon & Wed-Fri, 10-3pm Sat & Sun Ⓜ Panepistimio

See how folks did things 'way back when' at the Museum of Greek Folk Art (p31)

Get some ancient fashion tips at the Benaki Museum (p19)

Mon & Thu-Sat, 9am-9pm Wed, 11am-4pm Sun Ⓜ Akropoli

Epigraphical Museum (4, D2)

This museum, on the site of the National Archaeological Museum, houses the world's most important collection of Greek inscriptions. It is in effect a 'library of stones' detailing official records, lists of war dead, tribute lists showing annual payments by Athens' allies, and the decree ordering the evacuation of Athens before the 480 BC Persian invasion.
☎ 210 821 7637 🖳 www .culture.gr ✉ Tositsa 1, Exarhia € free 🕑 8.30am-3pm Tue-Sun Ⓜ Viktoria ♿ good

Ilias Lalaounis Jewellery Museum (5, C6)

The talents of Greece's renowned jeweller are show-cased in this private museum. Pieces are inspired by various periods in Greek history and displays demonstrate ancient art from prehistoric times. Videos explain the jewellery-making process and gold-smiths demonstrate ancient and modern techniques. Tours in English available.
☎ 210 922 1044 🖳 www .lalaounis-jewelrymuseum .gr ✉ Kallisperi 12 (cnr Kary-atidon), Makrigianni € €4, admission free 3-9pm Wed & 9-11am Sat 🕑 9am-4pm

Islamic Art Museum (5, A3)

The Benaki Museum's celebrated collection of Islamic art is one of the finest in the world. This stately neoclassical complex of buildings exhibits more than 8000 items covering the 12th to 19th century, including weavings, carvings, prayer carpets, tiles, ceramics and a 17th-century reception room from a Cairo mansion.
☎ 210 325 1311 🖳 www .benaki.gr ✉ Agion Asomaton 22 (cnr Dipylou), Keramikos € €5/3, admis-sion free Wed 🕑 9am-3pm Tue & Thu-Sun, 9am-9pm Wed Ⓜ Thisio

Jewish Museum (11, C2)

One of the most important in Europe, this modern museum traces the history of the Romaniote and Shephardic Jewish community in Greece from the 3rd century BC. The impressive collection includes religious and historical artefacts, documents, folk art and costumes. Nearly 90% of Greece's Jews, most of who lived in Thessaloniki, were killed during the Holocaust.

GOING UNDERGROUND

Even if you don't plan to board a train, a visit to one of Athens' splendid metro stations is a must. Construction of the underground rail network turned into Greece's biggest archaeological dig. Graves, foundations of ancient structures, ancient wells and thous-ands of artefacts were found, causing major delays. Many metro stations are now mini-museums, with excellent displays at Syntagma, Akropoli and Evangelismos. All stations also have major art installations by leading Greek artists, such as Alekos Fassianos's work at Metaxourgio station, Yiannis Gaïtis's trademark little men at Larisis and New York–based artist Stephen Antonakos's neon installation at Evangelismos.

☎ 210 322 5582 🖳 www
.jewishmuseum.gr ✉ Nikis
39, Plaka € €5/2 ⏲ 9am-
2.30pm Mon-Fri, 10am-2pm
Sun Ⓜ Syntagma

Kanellopoulos Museum (11, A2)

The imposing 1884 mansion
on the northern slope of the
Acropolis houses the Kanellopoulos family's extensive
collection, donated to the
state in 1976. After a major
refurbishment and expan-
sion, it was due to open by
2007. The collection includes
jewellery, clay-and-stone
vases and figurines, weapons,
Byzantine icons, bronzes and
objets d'art dating from every
period of Greek history.
☎ 210 321 2313 ✉ Theo-
rias 12 (cnr Panos), Plaka
€ €3 ⏲ 8.30am-3pm
Tue-Sun Ⓜ Monastiraki

Museum of Greek Costume (5, E3)

Part of the Lyceum of Greek
Women, this museum
presents excellent thematic
exhibitions from its comprehensive collection of regional
costumes, jewellery and
accessories. There are also 23
porcelain dummies in traditional dress that belonged
to Queen Olga. The gift shop
sells interesting books on folk
culture, as well as calendars
and handmade crafts.
☎ 210 362 9513
✉ Dimokritou 7, Kolonaki
€ free ⏲ 10am-2pm
Mon-Fri, 5-10pm Thu, closed
Aug Ⓜ Syntagma

Museum of Greek Folk Art (11, C3)

This state-owned museum
founded in 1918 moved
to Plaka in 1973. It has

examples of folk art from
1650 to the present,
including elaborate embroi-
dery, weaving, costumes,
shadow-theatre puppets,
silverwork, and wood and
stone carvings. The 1st floor
has fine wall murals by
renowned primitive artist
Theophilos Hatzimichail,
and a temporary exhibition
gallery. A new **annexe** (11,
A2; Panos 22) focuses on
Man and Tools.
☎ 210 322 9031 🖳 www
.culture.gr ✉ Kydathineon
17, Plaka € €2 ⏲ 9am-
2pm Tue-Sun Ⓜ Syntagma

Museum of Greek Popular Instruments (11, A2)

More than 1200 folk instruments dating from the 18th
century are on display over
three floors, with head-
phones allowing visitors
to listen to the music of
the *gaida* (Greek goatskin
bagpipes) and Byzantine
mandolins, among others.

The 1842 mansion is home
to the Research Centre for
Ethnomusicology and its
extensive archives. Recitals of
Greek music are often held in
the garden.
☎ 210 325 0198 🖳 www
.culture.gr ✉ Diogenous
1-3, Plaka € free ⏲ 10am-
2pm Tue & Thu-Sun, noon-
6pm Wed Ⓜ Monastiraki

Museum of Traditional Greek Ceramics (11, A1)

An annexe of the Museum of
Greek Folk Art, this museum
features folk pottery and
hand-painted ceramics from
the first two decades of the
20th century, collected by
professor Vassilil Kyriazop-
oulos. It is housed in the
mosque *(tzami)* built by the
city's governor, Tzisdarakis,
in 1759 (its minaret has been
removed).
☎ 210 324 2066 ✉ Areos
1, Monastiraki € €2
⏲ 9am-2.30pm Mon &
Wed-Sun Ⓜ Monastiraki

Lyres at the Museum of Greek Popular Instruments

Heads or tails? Old Roman coins, Numismatic Museum

Museum of Traditional Pottery (5, A3)

This small museum in a lovely neoclassical building around the corner from the Keramikos site is dedicated to the history of more contemporary (relatively) Greek pottery. A selection of ceramics from the museum's 4500-plus collection is on display and there is a reconstruction of a traditional potter's workshop. The centre holds periodic exhibitions and has a small gift shop.

☎ 210 331 8491 ✉ Melidoni 4-6, Keramikos € €3 ☽ 9-3pm Mon-Fri, 10am-2pm Sat Ⓜ Thisio

National Historical Museum (5, D3)

Since 1962 Greece's first parliament has housed memorabilia from the War of Independence, including Byron's helmet and sword, weapons, costumes and flags. There are also paintings, Byzantine and medieval exhibits, photos, and royal portraits illustrating Greece's evolution since Constantinople's fall in 1453.

☎ 210 323 7617 ✉ Stadiou 13, Plateia Kolokotroni € €3, admission free Sun ☽ 9am-2pm Tue-Sun Ⓜ Syntagma

Nautical Museum of Greece (3, C3)

This expansive museum brings Greece's maritime history to life, with models of ancient and modern ships, seascapes by some of Greece's greatest 19th- and 20th-century painters, and guns, flags and maps. There are also machine guns from old warships, anchors and part of a submarine on the museum's grounds.

☎ 210 451 6264 ✉ Akti Themistokleous, Freatida Sq, Marina Zea € €3 ☽ 9am-2pm Tue-Sat Ⓜ Piraeus, then bus 904 ⓐ good

Numismatic Museum (5, E3)

Even if you have no interest in coins, it is worth visiting this exemplary neoclassical building, once the home of renowned archaeologist Heinrich Schliemann, who excavated Troy and Mycenae. There are some beautiful frescoes and mosaic floors, and the museum's 600,000-strong collection is considered one of the top five in the world.

☎ 210 364 3774 ✉ Panepistimiou 12, Syntagma € €3 ☽ 8.30am-3pm Tue-Sun Ⓜ Syntagma ⓐ good

Philatelic Museum (5, F6)

Stamp collectors will love this small museum, featuring the history of philately and post offices in Greece. Exhibits range from old mailboxes and scales to postmen's uniforms and the 1886 printing plates from the first stamp, featuring a bust of Hermes, designed by the Hellenic Postal Service – and, naturally, a huge stamp collection.

☎ 210 751 9066 ✉ Fokianou 2, Plateia Stadiou, Mets € free ☽ 8am-2pm Ⓜ Syntagma ⍾ 2, 4, 11

Piraeus Archaeological Museum (3, C3)

This museum showcases antiquities from Piraeus, Attica, the Saronic Gulf and the island of Kythera, including finds from a Minoan sanctuary on Kythera. Star attractions are the four colossal bronzes, including a life-sized 520 BC statue of Apollo.

☎ 210 452 1598 ✉ Harilaou Trikoupi 31, Piraeus € €3 ☽ 8.30am-3pm Tue-Sun ⍾ 040 from Syntagma ⓐ excellent

War Museum (6, A3)

The junta-era museum honouring the armed forces has fighter planes in the forecourt that you can climb into. Inside, there is an invaluable historical collection of war memorabilia from the Mycenaean period to the present, including weapons, maps, armour and models of battles.

☎ 210 724 4464 ✉ Rizari 2 (cnr Vas Sofias) € free ☽ 9am-2pm Tue-Sun Ⓜ Evangelismos ⓐ good

NOTABLE BUILDINGS & MONUMENTS

Athens Town Hall (5, C2)
The 1874 town hall was abandoned for modern premises in the early 1980s, but following a major restoration the mayor's office moved back in 1995. The chambers have stunning frescoes by leading artists Kondoglou and Gounaropoulos, and also display a valuable collection of art.
☎ 210 331 2420/2
🖳 www.cityofathens.gr
✉ Athinas 63 (opposite Plateia Kotzia) € free
🕙 8am-3pm Ⓜ Omonia

Gennadius Library (6, B2)
In 1922 businessman turned diplomat John Gennadius handed over his personal library of books on Greece (more than 27,000 volumes) to the American School of Classical Studies. The fine neoclassical library has a stunning reading room and a fine art and memorabilia collection.
☎ 210 721 0536 🖳 www .ascsa.edu.gr/gennadius /genn.htm ✉ Souidias 61,

Kolonaki € free 🕙 9am-4.30pm Mon-Thu, 9am-3pm Fri, also 9am-2pm Sat in winter Ⓜ Evangelismos

Melina Mercouri Cultural Centre (7, C3)
Housed in the former Poulopoulou hat factory, this centre holds regular photography and cultural exhibitions. Its permanent exhibition is a re-creation of an Athenian street in 1900, with houses, shop windows and a *kafeneio* (coffee house).
☎ 210 345 2150 ✉ Iraklidon 66 (cnr Thessalonikis), Thisio € free 🕙 9am-1pm & 5-9pm Tue-Sat, 9am-1pm Sun Ⓜ Thisio ♿ good

National Theatre of Greece (5, B1)
Designed by Ernst Ziller and completed in 1901. The columned façade was inspired in part by Hadrian's Library; the interior was based on Vienna's People's Theatre. It served as the Royal Theatre exclusively for the king's guests until 1908. It was damaged in the 1999 earthquake and closed for renovation. It was expected to reopen in 2007. For performance details, see p83.

☎ 210 522 0585 🖳 www .n-t.gr ✉ Agiou Konstantinou 22, Omonia Ⓜ Omonia

Presidential Palace & Megaron Maximou (5, F4)
The imposing former royal palace designed by Ernst Ziller in the 1870s, guarded by two *evzones* (presidential guards), is now the official residence of the president of the Hellenic Republic. The prime minister's official residence, the Megaron Maximou, is an elegant neoclassical building down the road, regularly guarded by a media throng. Admission by invitation only.
✉ Irodou Attikou
Ⓜ Syntagma

Turkish Baths (11, A2)
This is the only surviving public bathhouse in Athens and one of the few remnants of the Ottoman period. The refurbished 17th-century bathhouse of Abit Efendi gives some insight into the era's rituals. Bathhouses were an important meeting point. There's a comprehensive audio guide.
☎ 210 3244340
✉ Kyristou 8, Plaka € €2
🕙 10am-2.30pm Tue-Sun
Ⓜ Monastiraki

BUILDING BOOM

This Akadimias trilogy is part of the legacy of the Hansen brothers, Theophile and Christian, Danish architects who joined the neoclassical building frenzy after independence.

Flanked by Apollo and Athena standing on two giant columns, the **Athens Academy** (5, D2) is considered Theophile's most impressive work in Greece. Completed in 1885, the exquisite frescoes in the entrance depict the myth of Prometheus.

The ostentatious buildings were built using white Pentelic marble and incorporate highly decorative friezes. The more modest senate house of the **Athens University** (5, D) in the middle was designed by Christian. Theophile's staircase of griffins leads to the 1902 **National Library** (5, D2; ☎ 210 338 2541; Panepistimiou 28-32, Panepistimio; 🕙 9am-8pm Mon-Thu, 9am-2pm Fri & Sat), which has a stunning reading room.

BYZANTINE CHURCHES & MONASTERIES

Agios Nicholas Rangavas (11, B3)

The 11th-century Byzantine church was part of the palace of the Rangava family, which included Michael I, emperor of Byzantium. The church bell was the first installed in Athens after liberation from the Turks (who banned them) and was the first to ring in 1833 to announce the freedom of Athens. It now hangs inside the church and is rung every year on 25 March.

☎ 210 322 8193 ✉ Prytaniou 1 (top of Epimarchou) ☾ 8am-noon & 5-8pm Ⓜ Akropoli

Athens Cathedral & Little Metropolis (11, B1)

The ornate 1862 Athens Cathedral dominates the square on Mitropoleos,

Church of the Holy Apostles

and is the archiepiscopal Greek Orthodox church of Athens. However, far more significant, both historically and architecturally, is the small 12th-century Church of Panagia Gorgoepikoos (Virgin Swift to Hear) next to the cathedral. Known as Little Metropolis, the cruciform-style church was built from marble, and used reliefs and pieces of ancient and early Christian monuments. It is also known as the Church of Agios Eleftherios, and is built on the ruins of an ancient temple.

☎ 210 322 1308 ✉ Plateia Mitropoleos, Monastiraki ☾ 7am-7pm, Sunday Mass 6.30am Ⓜ Monastiraki

Church of the Holy Apostles of Solakis (5, B4)

One of the oldest churches in Athens, built c AD 1000, this Byzantine church is on the site of the Ancient Agora. During the period of Ottoman rule it underwent many changes, but was restored in the 1950s. The church contains frescoes transferred from the demolished Agion Spyridon.

✉ Ancient Agora ☾ 8am-7pm Tue-Sun Apr-Nov, 8.30am-3pm Dec-Mar Ⓜ Monastiraki, Thisio

Dafni Monastery (1, A2)

One of the most splendid Byzantine monuments in Greece. The 11th-century Dafni Monastery's mosaics are considered masterpieces. Its closure, after damage caused by the 1999 earthquake, was the last in a long history of blows for the monastery – it's been sacked by crusaders, desecrated by Turks, occupied by Gothic Cistercian monks, destroyed by antipagan emperors' edicts and later turned into a barracks and mental institution. Restoration works were still going at the time of writing and it was unclear when it would reopen.

☎ 210 581 1558 ✉ Iera Odos, Haidari ☾ closed 🚌 A16 from Koumoundourou Sq

Kaisariani Monastery (1, B2)

The 11th-century monastery of Kaisariani, nestled on the

slopes of Mt Hymmetos, is a peaceful and green sanctuary only 5km from the city. Athenians once came here to drink from the 'magical' springs to aid fertility. Four columns from the ancient temple support the dome of the cruciform church, which has some well-preserved 17th- and 18th-century frescoes. The walled complex has a central court around which are the kitchen and dining rooms, the monks' cells and the bathhouse (all closed after being damaged in the 1999 earthquake). In its heyday the monastery had 300 monks.

☎ 210 723 6619
✉ mountain road starting at Ethnikis Antistaseos, Kaisariani € €2 ☼ monastery 8.30am-2.45pm Tue-Sun, grounds sunrise-sunset 🚌 20min trip 🚌 223 or 224 from Akadimias, then 2km uphill walk

Kapnikarea (11, B1)
Right in the middle of the pedestrian shopping strip of Ermou is the Byzantine church of Kapnikarea, dedicated to the Presentation of the Virgin Mary. Completed in the 13th century, the cruciform-style domed church was nearly destroyed to make way for progress. It now belongs to Athens University, which undertook its restoration.

☎ 210 322 4462
✉ Kapnikareas (cnr Ermou), Monastiraki ☼ 8am-1pm Mon, Wed & Sat, 8am-1pm & 4-8pm Tue, Thu & Fri, 8-11.30am Sun Ⓜ Monastiraki

Panagia Grigoroussa, Taxiarhon & Fanouriou (11, A1)
Every Saturday afternoon, worshippers arrive at this Plaka landmark for a special service to get their *fanouro-pita* (special spiced raisin cake) blessed before sharing it with passers-by. The cake is supposed to help you find something lost or someone you may be seeking. It tastes pretty good too.

✉ cnr Taxiarhon & Epaminonda (near Andrianou), Monastiraki ☼ 5.45pm Apr-Oct, 4.45pm Nov-Mar Ⓜ Monastiraki

Kaisariani Monastery

Sotira Lykodimou (11, C2)
The largest medieval structure (and only octagonal Byzantine church) in Athens has served as the Russian Orthodox Church since 1847. Built in 1031, it was bought and restored by Tsar Nicholas 1 in the 1850s while, at the end of the 19th century, Tsar Alexander II added the belfry.

✉ Filellinon (near Kydathineon) ☼ 7am-10am Ⓜ Syntagma

Find what you are looking for at the Panagia Grigoroussa, Taxiarhon & Fanouriou

ART MUSEUMS & GALLERIES

A.Antonopoulou.Art
(5, B2)

An impressive art space run by Angeliki Antonopoulou, who's been in the gallery business for years. Designed by leading architect Aris Zampikos, the gallery has great views of Psiri and focuses on contemporary Greek artists.

☎ 210 321 4994 🖥 aaart @otenet.gr ✉ 4th fl, Aristofanous 20, Psiri € free 🕑 4-9pm Tue-Fri, noon-4pm Sat Ⓜ Monastiraki

Atelier Spyros Vassiliou
(5, B6)

The home and studio of renowned Greek artist Spyros Vassiliou in a house near the Acropolis has been converted into a museum and archive dedicated to his work and life. The collection includes his portraits of Athens, theatre sets and artists tools.

☎ 210 923 1502 ✉ Webster 5a, Akropoli € 4 🕑 10am-8pm Mon-Fri, 10am-3pm Sat & Sun (closed mid-Aug) Ⓜ Thisio, Akropoli

Athens Municipal Art Gallery
(5, A2)

The municipality's rich collection includes more than 2300 works from the leading 19th- and 20th-century

Painting of a painter painting, National Art Gallery (p22)

Greek artists, with strong representation from the '30s generation, who created some of the masterpieces of Greek art. The gallery also boasts a fine collection of engravings.

☎ 210 324 3023 ✉ Pireos 51, Koumoundourou Sq € free 🕑 9am-1pm & 5-9pm Mon-Fri, 9am-1pm Sun Ⓜ Thisio

Bernier/Eliades Gallery
(7, C2)

This well-established gallery showcases artwork by prominent Greek artists and also brings exhibitions from an impressive range of international artists, from abstract American impressionists to British pop. It generally supports the younger generation of American and European artists.

☎ 210 341 3936 🖥 www .bernier-eliades.gr ✉ Eptahalkou 11, Thisio € free 🕑 10.30am-8pm Tue-Fri, noon-4pm Sat Ⓜ Thisio

Frissiras Museum
(11, C3)

This private museum of contemporary European paintings, in two beautifully renovated neoclassical mansions in Plaka, showcases more than 3000 works of art, focusing mainly on the human figure. The historic building at No 7 was designed by an unknown student of Ernst Ziller. There's a café.

☎ 210 323 4678 🖥 www .frissirasmuseum.com ✉ Monis Asteriou Tsangari 3 & 7, Plaka € €6 🕑 10am-5pm Wed-Fri, 11am-5pm Sat & Sun Ⓜ Syntagma ♿ good

Gazon Rouge
(4, B3)

Emerging artists from Greece and abroad are the focus of this hip gallery and art publishing house in a gritty but up-and-coming neighbourhood. There's a specialist book store and café on the ground level.

ART MAPS
Athens has a burgeoning contemporary arts scene. For a list of more than 50 city art galleries, complete with maps, go to www.athensartmap.net or www .artandthecity.gr or check out the Athens contemporary art review at www.athensbiennial.org.

☎ 210 524 8077 🖳 www
.gazonrouge.com ✉ Victor Hugo 15, Metaxourgio
€ free 🕑 noon-8pm
Tue-Fri, noon-4pm Sat
Ⓜ Metaxourgio

Herakleidon (7, C3)
Housed in a beautifully refurbished neoclassical building among the busy café strip in Thisio, this private museum has one of the world's most important collections of works by MC Escher. It hosts temporary international visual arts exhibitions. There's a great little café in the courtyard, and a gift shop.
☎ 210 346 1981 🖳 www
.herakleidon-art.gr ✉ Iraklidon 16, Thisio € €6
🕑 1pm-9pm, closed mid-Aug Ⓜ Thisio

Ileana Tounta Contemporary Art Centre (6, B1)
This leading gallery has two exhibition halls and an art shop, and it boasts one of Athens' trendiest restaurants. Tounta has an established record of hosting eclectic exhibitions by international and Greek artists.
☎ 210 643 9466 🖳 www
.art-tounta.gr ✉ Armatolon Ke Klefton 48, Lykavittos
€ free 🕑 11am-8pm Tue-Fri, noon-4pm Sat Ⓜ Ambelokipi 🚻 good

National Glyptoteque (1, B2)
The National Gallery's significant sculpture collection is now exhibited at this dedicated annexe located

in the historic former royal stables in Goudi. The permanent collection includes approximately 150 works from Greek artists of the 19th and 20th century, as well as international artists. It also hosts temporary exhibitions.
☎ 210 770 9855 🖳 www
.culture.gr ✉ Army Park, Katehaki € 6 🕑 5-10pm
Mon & Wed, 9am-3pm
Thu-Sat, 10am-3pm Sun
Ⓜ Katehaki 🚻 good

National Museum of Contemporary Art (4, B8)
The landmark former Fix brewery is being transformed into the capital's first comprehensive modern art museum, showcasing works by both Greek and foreign artists. Periodic exhibitions will be held in various venues around Athens until the art museum reopens after 2008. Check its website for further details.
☎ 210 924 2111/2
🖳 www.emst.gr ✉ Kaliroïs (cnr Frantzi), Fix
Ⓜ Syngrou-Fix 🚻 good

Pierides Museum of Contemporary Art (4, A1)
Dimitris Pierides founded this contemporary art museum, in a stunning mansion, for his collection of more than 1000 paintings, sculptures, engravings and ceramics, mostly by post-WWII artists from Greece and Cyprus. There's also a library of modern Greek art.
☎ 210 898 0166 ✉ Vasiliou Georgiou 29, Glyfada
€ free 🕑 9am-3pm Mon-Fri (6-8.30pm for special exhibitions), 10am-2pm Sat & Sun 🚋 5 🚌 A2 5th stop Glyfada

Catch a contemporary exhibit at Ileana Tounta

PARKS & PUBLIC PLACES

Athens First Cemetery (4, E8)

In a city with limited open space, the old cemetery is a pleasant, if quirky, place to enjoy a stroll through the well-tended gardens and resting place of rich and famous Greeks and philhellenes. The lavish tombstones include works of art by leading 19th-century sculptors, including *The Sleeping Maiden* by Halepas on the tomb of a young girl, and archaeologist Heinrich Schlieman's mausoleum with Trojan War scenes.

☎ 210 923 6118 ⊠ Anapafseo (cnr Trivonianou), Mets ☉ 7.30am-7pm May-Sep, 8am-5pm Oct-Apr 🚌 4

Athens Olympic Sports Complex (OAKA) (1, B2)

The vast complex of stadiums where the main action took place during the 2004 Olympics includes Santiago Calatrava's striking glass-and-steel roof and the futuristic shimmering Wall of Nations. You can wander through the site freely but the stadiums can only be visited on organised tours (per person €3; minimum of 15 people). Independent travellers can ask to join a tour (fax 210 683 4021 or email oakaprel@otenet.gr).

☎ 210 683 4777 🖳 www .oaka.com.gr ⊠ Marousi € free Ⓜ Irini ♿ excellent

Athinais (7, A1)

This modern arts and cultural complex is in an impressively restored early-20th-century silk factory. It hosts temporary art and historical exhibitions and has a cinema, music venue, theatre, café, arty gift shop and the well-regarded Red restaurant.

☎ 210 348 0000 🖳 www .athinais.com.gr ⊠ Kastorias 34-36, Votanikos € exhibitions €3 ☉ 9.30am-10pm 🚌 813 from Pireos, Omonia, to Sidera stop ♿ excellent

Areos Park (4, D1)

The city's biggest park, just north of the Archaeological Museum, can be a good place to escape the madness during the day. Among its wide tree-lined avenues is a long line of statues of War of Independence heroes. Avoid it at night, when it is frequented by vagrants and shady characters.

⊠ Alexandras (cnr 28 Oktovriou-Patission), Pedion Areos € free Ⓜ Viktoria ♿ good

Eleftherias Park Arts Centre (6, B2)

Among the small green oasis on this busy street, the old army barracks used as a prison during the junta era have been converted into two galleries used for temporary art exhibitions. The park is also home to a small museum dedicated to the great statesman Eleftherios Venizelos, and a pleasant café-restaurant.

☎ 210 723 2603 ⊠ Vas Sofias (Eleftherias Park), Ambelokipi € free ☉ 9am-1pm & 5-9pm Tue-Sat, 9am-1pm Sun, no exhibitions Jul & Aug Ⓜ Megaro Moussikis

National Gardens (5, E4)

The former royal gardens, designed by Queen Amalia around the palace that is now Parliament, are a great green refuge during the summer. Winding paths lead to ornamental ponds with waterfowl and a botanical museum, which

Waterfowls make a splash at the National Gardens

PANATHENAIC STADIUM

The imposing Panathenaic (or Panathenian) marble **stadium** (5, F6; ☎ 210 325 1744; www.culture.gr; Vas Konstantinou, Mets) was the venue for the first modern Olympic Games in 1896.

It was originally built in the 4th century BC to host the Panathenaic games. Under Hadrian's reign, it held gladiatorial contests – 1000 wild animals are said to have been slaughtered in the arena at his inauguration.

Athenian benefactor Herodes Atticus built a new stadium in Pentelic marble for the AD 144 Panathenaic Festival. In the 19th century it was completely restored by wealthy benefactor Georgios Averof to host the first modern Olympics. In 2004 the Kallimarmaron, as it is widely known, made a stunning backdrop to the archery competition and the marathon finish during the Athens Olympics. The public can no longer walk inside the site.

has interesting drawings, paintings and photographs. The café near Irodou Attikou is a pleasant rest spot. ☎ 210 721 5019 ✉ Amalias, Syntagma € free ⏰ 7am–dusk Ⓜ Syntagma ♿ good

Omonia Square (5, C1)
Once a grand square, these days Omonia is a hectic transport and business hub by day and hang-out for the city's seedier elements by night. It's had several transformation attempts but the architects just can't seem to get it right. After public outcry over the uninspiring concrete square unveiled in 2002, a few trees were added, but little else has been done since. ✉ Omonia Sq € free Ⓜ Omonia

Technopolis (7, B2)
This innovative cultural centre is in the superbly converted Athens 1862 gasworks complex. Old furnaces and other industrial features have been maintained, along with the different stone buildings from this once-thriving

self-sufficient community, including a carpenter's shop, smelter, garage, restaurant, barber and clinic. It hosts multimedia exhibitions, concerts and special events and the small **Maria Callas museum** (7, A2; ⏰ 10am–3pm Mon-Fri) dedicated to the revered opera diva. ☎ 210 346 0981 🖥 www .technopolis.gr ✉ Pireos 100, Gazi € free ⏰ during exhibitions 9am-9pm Mon-Fri Ⓜ Thisio ♿ good

Zappeio Gardens (5, E5)
The Zappeio's formal gardens surround the majestic palace

built in the 1870s by the wealthy Greek-Romanian benefactor Konstantinos Zappas, next to the National Gardens. It was used as the headquarters of the Olympic Committee for the 1896 Olympics, held opposite at the Panathenaic Stadium (see above). Unless there's a function on, the guards will let you in for a look at the stunning courtyard. The historic Aigli outdoor cinema (p93) and Cibus restaurant (p71) are next door. ✉ Amalias, Syntagma € free Ⓜ Syntagma ♿ good

Technopolis is all industrial art chic

QUIRKY ATHENS

Ancient Shipsheds (3, D3)
In the exposed basement of an ordinary Piraeus apartment block are the ruins of three slipways from an ancient shipshed. Zea was the main base for the Athenian fleet, which had more than 196 shipsheds (the ancients used to drag their ships in to shore). In a great example of preserving the past while getting on with life, the ruins can be seen next to the pylons holding up the building. It is lit at night and visible from the street.
✉ Sirangiou 1 (cnr Akti Moutsoupoulou), Piraeus
ⓔ free 🚍 20, Sirangiou stop ♿ good

Limni Vouliagmenis (1, B3)
The source of the water at this lake has never been found, as some divers have lost their lives discovering. But the lake is popular with winter swimmers who enjoy the constant 22°C temperature of part-salt/part-spring water, which has therapeutic mineral qualities. It's a wonderful setting, with its sheltered rock face, manicured lawns and old-style café-bar, frequented by a regular crew of elderly citizens in their bathrobes and bathing caps. Its gradual slope makes it good for kids.
☎ 210 896 2239 ✉ Limni Vouliagmeni ⓔ €7 ⏲ 7am-7.30pm summer, 7am-5pm winter 🚍 A2 (or E2 express in summer) to Plateia Glyfada, then bus 114

St John the Baptist of the Column (5, B2)
The name of this little church in downtown Athens comes from the incongruous Corinthian marble column that sticks out from the roof. While some believed it came from a gymnasium, another theory is that it once supported a Roman statue. The church (1844) was built around it during the Byzantine period, when it became a talisman believed to have magical healing properties. On 29 August people come here to perform a ritual from that time, when fever patients attached a waxed thread to the column to transfer the fever to the column.
✉ Evripidou (cnr Menandrou), Athens ⏲ 7am-3pm Ⓜ Monastiraki

HELLENIC COSMOS
Take a virtual reality trip into ancient Greece at this hi-tech interactive **museum** (7, A3; ☎ 210 483 5300; www.fhw.gr/cosmos; Pireos 254, Tavros; ⏲ summer 9am-4pm Mon, Tue & Thu, 9am-7pm Wed & Fri, 10am-3pm Sun; Ⓜ Kalithea); admission is free, though there's a fee for activities, and disabled access is excellent. Enter the Kivotos time machine – with floor-to-ceiling screens – and go back 2000 years to a 3D ancient Miletus, the Temple of Zeus at Olympia or the world of Greek costume.

There's a second 'magic screen' and at the time of writing a virtual reality cinema was set to open soon. The centre is part of the Foundation of the Hellenic World. English guides are available on request.

Tom's Garden (11, C2)
Tucked behind the main drag of Plaka, this temple to innovative and artistic recycling and political commentary has been making passers-by do a double take for years. The mysterious British refugee has turned a vacant lot into an ever-changing art display which, on last sight, had an elephant at the wheel of an old pink VW Beetle (Taliban Taxi Service).
✉ Sotiras (cnr Iperidou), Plaka ⓔ free Ⓜ Syntagma

You never know what you'll find at Tom's Garden

ATHENS FOR CHILDREN

Also look for the 🏃 icon in individual reviews in the Eating and Sleeping chapters.

Allou Fun Park

Giant entertainment zone with more than 20 amusement rides and occasional live shows. The **Kidom centre** next door is aimed at younger children and closes at midnight. Allou is about 7km west of downtown Athens.

☎ 210 425 6999 ✉ Kifissou (cnr Petrou Ralli), Renti €€ per attraction €2-5 ⏱ 5pm-2am Mon-Fri, 10am-2am Sat & Sun 🚃 21 to 3rd cemetery stop

Attica Zoological Park

Greece's only zoo has made a commendable effort to show Athenians a motley assortment of animals. It's a bit of a trek out near the airport.

☎ 210 663 4724 ✉ Yalou, Spata €€ adult/child aged 3-12 €11/9 ⏱ 9am-sunset) Ⓜ Doukissis Plakentias, bus 319 ♿ good

Battleship Averoff

Children will love climbing and exploring this restored battleship, now a museum. It was the fastest ship in the Greek fleet between 1910 and 1920. Visitors can tour the ship from the engine room to the captain's quarters.

☎ 210 983 6539 ✉ Trocadero Marina, Palio Faliro €€ €1 ⏱ 10am-1pm Mon-Fri & 6-8pm Mon, Wed & Fri; 3-5pm winter Ⓜ Syngrou-Fix, then bus 450 or 550, or tram Line 4 to Trocadero stop

Children's Art Museum (11, C2)

Founded to cultivate a love of art and creative development, this museum is one of the few of its kind. There are exhibitions of young artists' work and workshops for children.

☎ 210 331 2621 💻 www .childrensartmuseum.gr ✉ Kodrou 9, Plaka €€ adult/ child €2/free ⏱ 10am-2pm Tue-Sat, 11am-2pm Sun, closed Aug Ⓜ Syntagma

Children's Museum (11, C3)

This interactive centre has a range of activities to encourage children's development and engage the imagination, such as a popular chocolate-making session. Exhibits are in Greek only; some activities are suitable for non–Greek speakers, and staff speak English.

☎ 210 331 2995 💻 www .hcm.gr ✉ Kydathineon 14, Plaka €€ free ⏱ 10am-2pm Tue-Fri, 10am-3pm Sat & Sun (closed Jul & Aug) Ⓜ Syntagma

Goulandris Natural History Museum (8, B1)

The museum has comprehensive exhibits of animals and plant life, fossils and shells over two levels. The **GAIA Centre** around the corner focuses on the environment and evolution of the planet, with interactive displays for kids over 10; there's English audio commentary (€2).

☎ 210 801 5870 💻 goul@ gnhm.gr ✉ Levidou 13, Kifisia €€ museum €5/3, museum & GAIA Centre €7/4, child under 5 free ⏱ 9am-2.30pm Mon-Sat, 10am-2.30pm Sun, closed Aug Ⓜ Kifisia

Planetarium (Eugenides Foundation) (4, A9)

The 280-seat planetarium, with a 950-sq-metre hemispherical dome, has 3D virtual trips to the galaxy, as well as IMAX movies and other high-tech shows about ancient Greece. There is simultaneous narration in English (€1).

☎ 210 946 9641 💻 www .eugenfound.edu.gr ✉ Syngrou 387, Palio Faliro €€ digital shows €6/3, IMAX €8/5 ⏱ 5.30-8.30pm Wed-Fri, 10.30am-8.30pm Sat & Sun Ⓜ Syngrou-Fix then bus 550 or B2 to Onassio.

Railway Museum

Though not strictly for children, the collection of old steam locomotives, mine trains, wagons, royal carriages and trams here is sure to appeal to kids at heart. Highlights include an 1899 steam locomotive and passenger car from the famous rack railway of Diakofto–Kalavrita, and the smoking car of the train of Sultan Abdul Aziz.

☎ 210 524 6580 ✉ Liossion 301 & Siokou 4, Sepolia €€ free ⏱ 9am-1pm Fri-Sun Ⓜ Sepolia

Spathario Museum of Shadow Theatre

This exhibition of the famous Karaghiozi and his colourful band of shadow-theatre puppets was founded in 1965 by Eugene Spatharios. The collection dates back to 1947. There are also Greek and English books on shadow theatre.

☎ 210 612 7245 ✉ cnr Vas Sofias & Ralli (Kastalias Sq), Maroussi €€ free ⏱ 9am-2pm Mon-Fri, 6-8pm Wed Ⓜ Maroussi 🚌 A7, B7

WORTH THE TRIP

Cape Sounion

One of the most spectacular ancient sites in Greece, the **Temple of Poseidon** is perched on the craggy cliffs of Cape Sounion, 70km southeast of Athens. It is best appreciated early morning or late in the afternoon, when the tour buses have gone and you can enjoy the stunning sunsets. Built in the 5th century BC on the site of previous sanctuaries, this is where the ancient Greeks worshipped the god of the sea. Lord Byron carved his name in one of the columns in 1810. In summer you can stop along the coast for a swim.

☎ 22920 39363
🖳 www.culture.gr € €4

🕑 9.30am-sunset summer, 9.30am-5pm winter 🚍 from Mavromateon terminal (☎ 210 823 0179; cnr Alexandras & 28 Oktovriou-Patission), Areos Park

Eleusis (1, A2)

The sanctuary of Demeter was one of the most fascinating ancient places in Greece, site of cult worship and Eleusinian mysteries celebrating the goddess Demeter and her daughter Persephone. It's now in the middle of an industrial wasteland on the coast a one-hour bus ride, 22km west of Athens. The on-site museum has some significant finds and a good model of the site. It's been lit by French lighting expert Pierre Bideau, who did the Acropolis.

☎ 210 554 6019
🖳 www.culture.gr
✉ Gioka 1, Elefsina
€ €3 🕑 8am-7.30pm
🚍 Athens–Corinth Hwy to Elefsina 🚍 A16 or B16 from Koumoundourou Sq

Koutouki Cave (1, B2)

Although facilities at Koutouki Cave have seen better days, the cave itself – one of the finest in Greece – is a pleasant surprise. Discovered by a shepherd in 1926 after his goat fell down a hole, it was excavated and opened to the public. You can tour the two-million-year-old cave's stalactites and stalagmites (30-minute tours, every half-hour, complete with sound-and-light show finale).

☎ 210 664 2910
🖳 www.culture.gr

Magnificent Temple of Poseidon, a fitting place to worship the god of the sea

MOUNT PARNITHA

Just 20km north of the city centre, and a popular weekend escape for Athenians, lies **Mt Parnitha National Park** (1, B1).

Mt Parnitha itself comprises a number of smaller peaks, the highest of which is Mt Karavola at 1413m – high enough to get snow in winter. The park is criss-crossed by numerous walking trails, marked on the Road Editions trekking map. Most visitors access the park by cable car from the outer Athens suburb of Thrakomakedones. The cable car drops you below **Casino Mt Parnes** (☎ 210 242 1234; www.mont-parnes.gr; ☽ 24hr), a gaming and hotel complex that is being renovated and expanded.

The casino runs a free bus service from various locations in Athens, including outside the Hilton. You can get to the cable car station on bus 714 from the south end of Aharnon, near Omonia.

✉ Peania Cave € €5 ☽ 9am-3.50pm Ⓜ Ethniki Amyna, then by car or taxi for 4km

Marathon (1, C1)

The site of one of the most famous battles of all time – in which the outnumbered Athenians defeated the 25,000-strong Persian Army – is located about 4km before the town of Marathon. There's a memorial near the 10m burial mound (tumulus), a model of the battle as well as historical information. The excellent refurbished Marathon **museum** (☎ 229 405 5155) displays neolithic pottery from the Cave of Pan, finds from the tomb of the Athenians and recently discovered larger statues from a nearby Egyptian sanctuary. There are also two grave circle sites worth visiting on the way. The bus (KTEL; ☎ 210 823 0007; departs hourly from Mavromateon to Marahonos) stops about 350m from the site but the museum is a 2km walk from there, making getting there a bit tricky if you don't have access to a car.

☎ 229 405 5462 ✉ 114 Plateon, Marathonas € site & museum €3 ☽ 8.30am-3pm Tue-Sun 🚌 Marathonos from Mavromateon to Tymvos

Ramnous (1, C1)

The less visited, evocative and secluded site of Ramnous is located on a picturesque plateau overlooking the sea, around 10km northeast of Marathon. Among the ruins of Ramnous' ancient ports are the remains of the **Doric Temple of Nemesis** (435 BC), which once contained a huge statue of the goddess of retribution and mother of Helen of Troy. There are also ruins of a smaller 6th-century temple. About 1km down a picturesque track there is a relatively well-preserved fortress on the clifftop near the sea, with the remains of the city, a temple, gymnasium and theatre. There are coves nearby where you can enjoy a swim.
☎ 22940 63477 🖳 www.culture.gr ✉ Ramnous € €2 ☽ 8am-5.30pm

Vravrona (1, C2)

The Sanctuary of Artemis was a revered site for worshippers of the goddess of the hunt and protector of women in childbirth and newborns. The temple is one of several notable monuments from this Neolithic settlement. The museum houses exceptional finds from the sanctuary and excavations in the area.
☎ 22990 27020 🖳 www.culture.gr ✉ Vravrona € €3/1.50 ☽ 8.30am-3pm Tue-Sun Ⓜ Ethniki Amina, then bus 304 to Loutsa (1hr), then taxi 10min

Vorres Museum (1, B2)

This private modern art and folk museum is set on a lovely 2.5-hectare estate. Vorres built his home here in 1963 and began collecting art, furniture, artefacts, textiles and historic objects from around Greece to preserve the national heritage.
☎ 210 664 2520 🖳 www.culture.gr ✉ Parodos Diadohou Konstantinou 4, Peania € €4.50 ☽ 10am-2pm Sat & Sun & daily Aug, Tue-Fri by appointment Ⓜ Ethniki Amina, then bus 308 to Koropi-Peania

Trips & Tours

WALKING TOURS

For organised walking tours see p52.

Plaka

From **Parliament** (**1**; p16) walk along the National Gardens to the well-preserved **Roman Baths** (**2**; p18), and backtrack to cross Amalias and enter Plaka from Kydathineon. Stop at the **Museum of Greek Folk Art** (**3**; p31), opposite the Church of Metamorphosis.

Turn right at Adrianou, left at Flessa, and right again on Kyristou, past the **Turkish Baths** (**4**; p33), to the ingenious **Tower of the Winds** (**5**; p18).

Follow the **Roman Agora** (**6**; p18) around and head up the steps alongside the **Ancient Agora** (**7**; p17) where you can take in the views at Dioskouros café before continuing to the foot of the Acropolis.

Turn back along Theorias past the **Kanellopoulos Museum** (**8**; p31) to Agios Simeon Church. Walk around the back of the church (small opening on right), to get to the winding paths of the **Anafiotika quarter** (**9**; p13).

At the church of St George of the Rock, turn into the terraced park and walk out the gate down past Rangava. To your left the path leads to the Church of Agios Nicholas Rangavas. Turn right into Tripodon and the cute **Amalthia café** (**10**; Tripodon 16) or keep going until you get to the **Lysicrates Monument** (**11**; p25). Continue along Vyronos St to the Akropoli metro station or wander back through the streets of Plaka.

Ancient scrubbing at the Turkish Baths

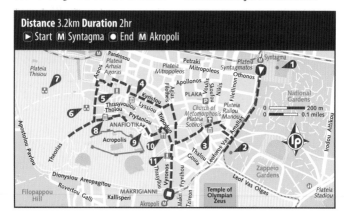

Distance 3.2km **Duration** 2hr
▶ Start Ⓜ Syntagma ⦿ End Ⓜ Akropoli

Ancient Promenade

From Monastiraki station, turn into Areos at the **old mosque (1)**, now the Museum of Traditional Greek Ceramics (p31), pass the imposing **Hadrian's Library (2**; p18) opposite the metro and then turn right into historic Adrianou, where Europe's longest pedestrian promenade begins. On your left you'll see the **Stoa of Attalos (3**; p17) and the **Temple of Hephaestus (4**; p17) in the **Ancient Agora (5**; p17). At Thisio station, turn left and continue along the wide promenade, which winds around the foothills of the Acropolis. Up on the hill below the Acropolis you will see people admiring the view from **Areopagus Hill (6)**. On your right you will see the old **Athens Observatory (7)** and the **Church of Agia Marina (8**; p23) and some recently excavated ruins.

Continue into Dionysiou Areopagitou towards the **Odeon of Herodes Atticus (9**; p26) where you can admire the Stoa of Eumenes that connects it with the **Theatre of Dionysos (10**; p26). In the wall of the Acropolis you will see the **sacred caves (11)**. Back on Dionysiou Areopagitou, the new **Acropolis Museum (12**; p12) is on your right as you head towards the end of the pedestrian precinct. Cross over busy Syngrou for a peek at **Hadrian's Arch (13**; p25) and the imposing **Temple of Olympian Zeus (14**; p25). Cross back towards the Akropoli metro station, or head down Lysikratous into Plaka.

Hadrian's Arch, now a window to the sky

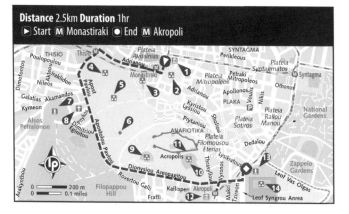

Distance 2.5km **Duration** 1hr
▶ Start Ⓜ Monastiraki ● End Ⓜ Akropoli

Athens Landmarks

Begin at **Parliament** (**1**; p16), about 10 minutes before the hour to catch the changing of the guard. Head south along the National Gardens, and turn left towards the **Zappeio palace** (**2**; p39). Continue through the gardens and cross the road to reach the **Panathenaic Stadium** (**3**; p39).

Backtrack and head up Irodou Attikou past the **Presidential Palace** (**4**; p33) and the **Megaron Maximou** (**5**; p33), the prime minister's residence, where you may see another mini changing of the guard ceremony. Turn left at Vas Sofias, which is lined with museums and embassies. Directly opposite is the excellent **Benaki Museum** (**6**; p19). Walk past Parliament and turn right into Panepistimiou, Athens' most impressive boulevard of grand buildings. You will pass the stunning **Numismatic Museum** (**7**; p32), St Denis Catholic Cathedral and the unusual 1847 Byzantine-style Eye Hospital.

Statues of Apollo and Athena stand on towering columns above the **Athens Academy** (**8**; p33), part of the neoclassical trilogy comprising the **Athens University** (**9**; p33) with the murals in the portico next door, and the marble-columned **National Library** (**10**; p33). Continue towards Omonia Sq (Plateia Omonias), crossing over into busy pedestrian Eolou, where you will see the Acropolis in the distance. The restored 1874 **Athens Town Hall** (**11**; p33) is on the other side of historic Plateia Kotzia, where you can see parts of the old walls of Athens under the new **National Bank building** (**12**; Eolou).

The colourful **Athens Central Market** (**13**; p54) is worth a detour. Continue along Eolou, past two churches before emerging at the Ermou shopping mall or continuing into Monastiraki.

Distance 4.2km **Duration** 2hr
- ▶ Start Ⓜ Syntagma
- ● End Ⓜ Monastiraki

Go nuts at Athens Central Market

Keramikos & Athens Hills

From Thisio metro, head towards the small Byzantine church of **Agion Asomaton** (**1**) near the start of the Ermou pedestrian precinct. On the right are the ruins of **Keramikos** (**2**; p27), and the excellent **Oberlaender Museum** (**3**; p27). Cross the stone bridge into Thisio (on Sunday there's a flea market just before the bridge) and head alongside the railway line until you get to the old hat factory that is now the **Melina Mercouri Cultural Centre** (**4**; p33), where you can see a free exhibition of old Athens. Head up Iraklidon towards the busy café strip, turn into Amfiktionos and walk until you get to the **Church of Agia Marina** (**5**; p23). The paved road behind the church leads to the **Old Athens Observatory** (**6**; p23), past which signposted steps lead up the hill to the **Pnyx theatre** (**7**; p23) which has spectacular views over Athens (gates close at 6pm).

A path past the theatre leads to the **Church of Agios Dimitrios Loumbardiaris** (**8**; p23); there's a pleasant café. From the church, a path leads up to the **Monument of Filopappos** (**9**; p23) on the summit, with views of the Acropolis and sea. Head back down to the pedestrian promenade, crossing over towards the **Acropolis** (**10**; p10). Further along are the steps leading to the **Areopagus** (**11**) lookout. A gate to right of the marble steps leads you through the outer (free) part of the **Ancient Agora** (**12**; p17) into Plaka, then past the **Roman Agora** (**13**; p18) into Monastiraki.

ATHENS 400 BC

Go back in time with this innovative theme walk led by actors who take you back to a typical day in Athens 400 BC, an interactive and entertaining two-hour stroll (€22) around the Plaka and Acropolis. They sing, debate and play games, and it concludes with an ancient picnic snack. It's run by **Scoutway** (11, B3; ☎ 210 321 1866; www .scoutway.gr; Adrianou 105 & Kekropos, Plaka; ⊙ 11am-9pm).

Distance 3km **Duration** 1½hr
▶ Start Ⓜ Thisio ● End Ⓜ Monastiraki

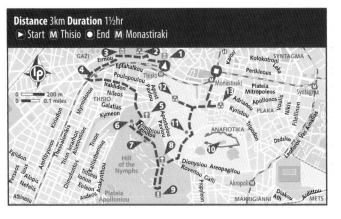

DAY TRIPS
Delphi (2, B1)

The ancient Greeks regarded Delphi as the centre of the world; according to mythology, Zeus released two eagles at opposite ends of the world and they met here at Delphi.

INFORMATION

178km northwest of Athens

- 🚌 Terminal B Liossion 260 (☎ 210 831 7096, €11, 3hr)
- ☎ museum 226 508 2312
- 🖥 www.culture.gr
- € €6
- 🕐 site & museum in summer 7.30am-6.30pm Tue-Sun, noon-6.30pm Mon; winter hours not available at the time of writing
- 🛈 Delphi tourist office (☎ 226 508 2900; Vas Pavlos & Fredirikis; 🕐 7.30am-2.30pm Mon-Fri); hire a car or take an organised tour

Divine inspiration at the Sanctuary of Apollo

When you stand at the **Sanctuary of Apollo** in its spectacular clifftop setting, you get a sense that this is indeed a special place. Pilgrims once came here (around the 4th century BC) seeking the wisdom of Apollo's oracle, thought to be literally the mouthpiece of the god.

In ancient times the **Sacred Way** was lined with treasuries and statues given by grateful city states in thanks to Apollo for helping them win battles.

These days the visitors are mostly tourists exploring the sanctuary and expansive archaeological sites. Ancient Delphi managed to amass a considerable treasure-trove, and this is reflected in the refurbished **museum**, which has an excellent collection of finds from the site, including the celebrated life-sized bronze charioteer whose piercing eyes follow you around the room.

If you come to Delphi by car, make time to visit the nearby skiing village of <u>Arachova</u> or head down to the seaside village of **Galaxidi** for fresh fish at one of the seafront tavernas (about 30 minutes' drive).

WINE TOURS

Wine tourism is still in its infancy but the **Attica Wine Growers Association** (☎ 210 353 1315; www.enoaa.gr) provides information and organises tours of local wineries participating in the Wine Roads of Attica programme.

The 30-hectare **Ktima Evharis** (☎ 210 924 6930, 229 609 0346; www.evharis.gr; Megara; 🕐 9am-4pm Mon-Fri, weekends by appointment), 64km from Athens, is one of the best visitor-friendly wineries near Athens. It offers tastings and tours, and has an extensive modern-art collection.

Nafplio (2, C2)

Tucked below the imposing cliff-top Palamidi Venetian fortress, the seaside town of Nafplio is one of Greece's most picturesque.

Briefly the capital of Greece during the War of Independence, Nafplio has been a major port since the Bronze Age. Its heritage-protected **old quarter** is a charming mix of Greek, Venetian and Turkish architecture, and it's full of cafés, restaurants and some great stores. The port is lined with stunning **neoclassical buildings**.

The main fortress, **Palamidi**, is an 800-step climb or a short taxi ride up and has spectacular views of the Gulf of Argos. There are also two other fortresses nearby. The smaller **Akronafplia** rises above the old town and is the oldest fortress, and the diminutive **Bourtzi** is on an islet west of the old town.

There are a number of museums worth visiting, including the Archaeological Museum, housed in an impressive stone building constructed by the Venetians at the beginning of the 18th century.

In June Palamidi hosts a **folk music festival**.

The ruins of **Tiryns**, 4km northwest of Nafplio, are also worth visiting. Tiryns was an important Mycenaean palace. Within the walls are vaulted galleries, secret stairways and storage chambers.

INFORMATION

146km southwest of Athens

- 🚌 Terminal A (Kifissou 100), departs on the hour
- ☎ Palamidi fortress 275 202 8036
- 🖳 www.culture.gr
- € Palamidi fortress €4
- 🕙 Palamidi fortress summer 8am-6.45pm, winter 8am-4.45pm
- ⓘ Nafplio tourist office (☎ 275 202 4444; 25 Martiou; 🕙 9am-1pm & 4-8pm)

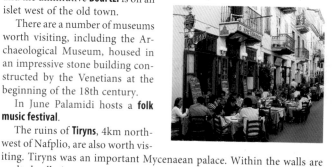

Island fortress of Bourtzi seen from Palamidi Fortress

Hydra (2, C3)

The island of Hydra, in the Saronic Gulf, is adored by artists and writers, and you can see why as soon as you enter the picturesque harbour. Gracious stone and whitewashed mansions line the surrounding hillside, forming a natural amphitheatre around the harbour.

INFORMATION

50km or 38 nautical miles from Piraeus

- Hellenic Seaways (☎ 210 419 9000) runs several daily high-speed services from Piraeus (one way €16.60, 1½hr), Piraeus Port Authority (☎ 210 412 4585) has a slower 3hr daily ferry at 8am
- ☎ Hydra tourist police 229 805 2205
- 🖵 www.hydra-island.com

It is a peaceful and charming island due to the absence of cars and motorbikes – donkeys are the only means of transport.

Most of the activity in Hydra is concentrated around the great waterfront cafés and shops, leaving the upper reaches virtually deserted. You can get pleasantly lost in the maze of winding streets.

The historic **Lazaros Kountouriotis mansion** on the hill has been turned into a wonderful museum under the auspices of the National Historical Museum and the **Nautical Museum** on the harbour is also worth a visit.

The rocky outcrop around **Hydronetta**, near the port, is popular for swimming; or you can take a pleasant walk to some small coves nearby.

Aegina (2, D3)

The closest island to Athens, Aegina makes for an easy and pleasant day trip. The boats arrive at Aegina town, with its long harbour, neoclassical buildings and busy cafés and shops. There are tavernas by the sea, north of the port, for lunch but the small fish-mezedopolia tucked in the fishmarket are an atmospheric, great value alternative. Regular buses go to the island's major ancient site, the splendid 480 BC **Temple of Aphaia**, on the way to the main beach town, **Agia Marina**.

INFORMATION

30km or 17 nautical miles from Piraeus

- daily ferries from Piraeus (one way €5, 1hr 10min); Hellenic Seaways (☎ 210 419 9000; www.hellenicseaways.gr) runs high-speed catamarans (one way €10, 35min)
- ☎ tourist police 229 702 7777
- 🖵 www.aeginagreece.com

ORGANISED TOURS
Classic Tours
Athens' main organised-tour companies offer almost identical similar services and normally cater to package tourists. Day tours usually involve a drive-by tour of the sights stopping at one or two key places such as the Acropolis and the museum.

Sights in Athens are easy to get to on your own so, in many cases, the only real advantage is the guide. The best regarded companies are **Chat** (11, C2; ☎ 210 323 0827; www.chatours.gr; Xenofontos 9, Syntagma), and **Hop In Sightseeing** (5, D6; ☎ 210 428 5500; www.hopin.com; Syngrou 19, Piraeus; ☺ 6.30am-10pm), which runs a Hop In–Hop Out tour that allows you to get on and off the bus over two days. Hop-In also does hotel pick-ups.

Sunshine Express (☎ 210 881 9252; www.sunshine-express.gr) runs the tourist train that departs from the Roman Agora (€5/3; hourly from 11.30am to midnight) and weaves through Plaka and the Thisio-Acropolis district.

The main tour companies also run half-day afternoon tours (€34) along the coastal road to the Temple of Poseidon at Cape Sounion (p42), as well as tours to Delphi (p48), Mycenae and the Corinth Canal, Nafplio (p49) and the ancient Theatre of Epidavros (p83). Most day trips cost around €80 to €90.

A couple of other tour companies include **GO Tours** (5, D6; ☎ 210 921 9555; Athanassiou Diakou 20, Makrigianni; ☺ 6am-9pm) and **Key Tours** (5, D6; ☎ 210 923 3166; www.keytours.gr; Kaliroïs 4, Mets; ☺ office 7am-8pm).

Archaeological Tours
With prior notice, the **Panhellenic Guides Federation** (☎ 210 322 9705; fax 210 323 9200; Apollonos 9A) can organise private tours by accredited guides (four hours about €90) to archaeological sites.

Classicist Andrew Farrington leads **Athenian Days** (☎ 210 864 0415, 697 766 0798; www.atheniandays.co.uk), which has private tailor-made cultural and historical introductions to the city (four to five hours, four to five persons) and day-long tours to surrounds (up to six people per tour). Prebooking essential.

Tour guide **Rania Vassiliadou** (☎ 210 940 3932; http://raniavassiliadou .virtualave.net) provides a well-regarded service around Athens' archaeological sites, and day trips further afield for up to six people.

DIY TOURS
One way to get around the sites is on the **Athens Sightseeing Public Bus Line** (☎ 185; www.oasa.gr; 🚌 400), which covers 20 key locations, from the National Archaeological Museum (p14) to the markets and ancient sites. Buses run half-hourly between 7.30am and 9pm; tickets (€5) can only be purchased on board. Tickets are valid for 24 hours and can be used on all public transport, excluding the airport services.

Boat Trips

Day cruises to the nearby islands of Hydra (p50), Poros and Aegina (p50) usually include a buffet lunch and onboard entertainment with traditional dancing. **Chat** (11, C2; ☎ 210 323 0827; www.chatours.gr; Xenofontos 9, Syntagma) offers a one-day cruise (€88) which stops at Hydra first, with time for a stroll or swim, and sails to Aegina, where for an extra charge you can take an excursion to the Temple of Aphaia.

Hop In Sightseeing (5, D6; ☎ 210 428 5500; www.hopin.com; Syngrou 19, Piraeus; ☷ 6.30am-10pm) does the same route in reverse (€90).

Walking Tours

City Walking Tours (☎ 210 884 7269; www.athenswalkingtours.gr; €29) offers several walking tours around the city from the markets to the archaeological sites.

For an alternative experience try the ancient Greece theme walk run by **Scoutway** (11, B3; ☎ 210 321 1866; www.scoutway.gr; Adrianou 105 & Kekropos, Plaka; ☷ 11am-9pm), walks by **Trekking Hellas** (11, C2; ☎ 210 331 0323; www.outdoorsgreece.com; Filellinon 7, Plaka) or do it yourself (p44).

Alternative Tours

Part-owned by the Scouts Association of Greece, **Scoutway** (11, B3; ☎ 210 321 1866; www.scoutway.gr; Adrianou 105 & Kekropos, Plaka; ☷ 11am-9pm) offers unique private tours and day trips, from Athens nightlife to the ancient mines at Lavrio or bungee jumping on the Corinth Canal. Most of the tours combine sightseeing with outdoor activities, such as hikes on nearby Hymettos and the Kaisariani Monastery (p34), mountain biking on Mt Parnitha (p43) or a trip to Corinth's ancient harbour, followed by canoeing.

Trekking Hellas (11, C2; ☎ 210 331 0323; www.outdoorsgreece.com; Filellinon 7, Plaka) runs various activities from an Athens walking tour (€37) to culinary theme walks.

Pretty as a picture; the waterfront and town behind Poros Harbour

Shopping

Shopping is a favourite Athenian pastime and the past few years have seen major retail development throughout Athens. The shopping scene is far more sophisticated now, and the somewhat disproportionate number of stores rather mind-boggling.

There are plenty of options for shopaholics, from exquisitely made shoes and jewellery, traditional handicrafts, big-name brands and designers to the latest streetwear designs.

The most concentrated mainstream strip is on pedestrian Ermou, from Syntagma to Monastiraki, which must have more shoes per square metre than anywhere in the world.

The new Attica department store and exclusive labels that are found in the Citylink shopping centre form the new gateway to the chic boutiques scattered around Kolonaki. Voukourestiou is lined with elite designers and jewellers.

Kifisia and Glyfada have great shopping and designer stores in a more relaxed environment. The big new arrival for the burbs is the Mall – a massive American-style shopping centre complex in the northern suburb of Marousi.

The tourist and gift stores in Plaka and Monastiraki open until late, meaning you can fit in a full day of sightseeing followed by dinner and still have time to buy souvenirs or spoil yourself with a unique piece of Greek jewellery. Opening hours are listed in reviews only where they deviate from the standard hours listed in the boxed text below.

The following guide is by no means definitive but suggests a broad range of interesting stores.

Be warned, some sales assistants can be in your face, greeting you with a terse *'parakalo'*, (a 'can I help you?' equivalent with a 'what do you want?' tone) and following you around the store. That said, most are friendly, speak English and are happy to assist.

During sale times (July to August and January to February) there are some great bargains. Haggling is only acceptable (and effective) in smaller, owner-run souvenir and jewellery stores (especially if you pay cash).

SHOPPING HOURS

Trading hours in Athens are still influenced by the old days when people went home for lunch and a siesta during the heat of the day. The family-run shops reopened in the evenings, which is still the best time to shop in summer. But times are changing and many stores now open through lunch, especially in central Athens and main shopping precincts.

Official trading hours are as follows: Monday, Wednesday and Saturday 9am to 3pm; Tuesday, Thursday and Friday 9am to 2.30pm and 5.30pm to 8.30pm (in winter 5pm to 8pm). Most department stores open Monday to Friday 8am to 8pm, and Saturday 9am to 6pm.

These hours do not apply to shops in busy tourist strips, like Plaka, which stay open until late (around 11pm).

Note that opening hours are listed in reviews only where they deviate from the standard hours given here.

DEPARTMENT STORES

Attica (5, E3)
The flashiest new shopper's magnet in downtown Athens, this high-end department store has eight levels of shopping, with leading brands, hip clothing, cosmetics and all sorts of temptations. It is part of the Citylink complex, which boasts some of the top fashion houses and jewellers, such as Dolce & Gabanna and Cartier.
☎ 211 180 2500 ✉ Panepistimiou 7, Syntagma 🕒 10am-9pm Mon-Fri, 10am-7pm Sat Ⓜ Syntagma

Fokas (11, C1)
This five-storey department store in a restored neoclassical building in the hub of Ermou stocks a select range of mens-, womens- and childrenswear labels, as well as travel goods, accessories, swimwear, beauty products, toys and books. There's a second store on Stadiou near Omonia.
☎ 210 325 7740 ✉ Ermou 11 (cnr Voulis), Syntagma Ⓜ Syntagma

Hondos Center (5, C1)
This major chain's 10-level superstore has just about everything, from designer clothes to sunscreen, plus an extensive range of swimwear, cosmetics and perfumes. The rooftop café has great views.
☎ 210 522 1335 ✉ Omonia Sq 4, Omonia Ⓜ Omonia

Notos Galleries (5, C1)
Boasting more than 400 shops in the one store, Notos Galleries nee Lambropoulos is one of Athens' oldest department stores, with Greek and imported labels in clothing, footwear, cosmetics and personal goods. There's also **Notos Galleries Home** (Plateia Kotzia), dedicated to furniture, kitchenware and other lifestyle products.
☎ 210 324 5811 ✉ Eolou 2-8, Omonia Ⓜ Omonia

MARKETS

Athens Central Market (5, C2)
The hectic, colourful Athens *agora* (market) is the highlight of the Athinas market strip. A visual and gastronomic delight with the most amazing range of olives, spices, cheeses and deli treats leads you to the meat market, which can look quite surreal, with hanging carcasses illuminated by endless rows of swinging light bulbs. The fresh fruit and vegetable market is nearby and there are some old-style tavernas (see Diporto Agoras, p76) close by too.

✉ Athinas (between Sofokleous & Evripidou), Omonia 🕒 7am-3pm Mon-Sat Ⓜ Omonia

Monastiraki Flea Market (5, B3)
Athens' traditional market is a scaled-down version of what it used to be, though is still has a festive atmosphere, with the nearby cafés and restaurants brimming on weekends. The permanent antique, furniture and collectables stores have plenty to sift through and are open all week.

✉ around Plateia Avyssinias, Monastiraki 🕒 antique stalls 8am-3pm, rest open till late Ⓜ Monastiraki

Piraeus Flea Market (3, C1)
This busy Sunday market spreads out along the streets around Piraeus railway station, with merchants selling everything from cheap clothing and shoes to tools and blankets. It is not strong on crafts; and for antiques and collectables, you're better off going during the week when you don't have to fight the crowds to get to the area's excellent antique shops.
✉ around Alipedou, Great Harbour, Piraeus 🕒 7am-2pm Sun Ⓜ Piraeus

Sunday Flea Market (7, B2)
This big market has moved to the end of Ermou, where traders peddle their stuff and you can find some bargains, interesting collectables and kitsch delights among the junk. This is the place to test your haggling skills.
✉ Keramikos 🕒 6am-2pm

Go on a see-food diet; prawns at the Athens Central Market

CLOTHING

Greek Designers

Bettina (5, F3)
This chic boutique has three levels of top-name fashion for all ages, including creations by international success story Sophia Kokosalaki, Angelos Frentzos and other well-known Greek and international designers.
☎ 210 323 8759 ✉ Pindarou 40 (cnr Anagnostopoulou), Kolonaki Ⓜ Syntagma

Christoforos Kotentos (5, B2)
Upstairs is the Psiri atelier of this hot, young local designer, whose clothing is sold in Milan, New York and Tokyo. Vasso Consola is also based in the same funky warehouse.
☎ 210 325 5434 ✉ Sahtouri 3, Psiri Ⓜ Monastiraki

Christos Veloudakis (5, F3)
A dramatic-looking boutique; the long red velvet curtains and racks of clothing are both designed for maximum impact. Women's and men's day- and nightwear with an edge.

Get hip at LAK

BREAKING THE FASHION BARRIER
Greek fashion has started to make a ripple in the international fashion scene, with a growing number of Greek designers showing on the catwalks of London, Milan, New York and Paris. Leading young designers include London-based Paris catwalk darling Sophia Kokosalaki, responsible for the stunning costumes in the Athens Olympics opening and closing ceremonies, Vasso Consola, Deux Hommes, Yiorgos Eleftheriades, Angelos Frentzos, Haris & Angelos, Lena Katsanidou, Christoforos Kotentos and Celia Kritharioti.

Local designers were in the international spotlight during the 2nd **Athens Fashion Week** in Athens in 2006, with the fashion extravaganza expected to become an annual event.

☎ 210 364 1764
✉ Tsakalof 22a, Kolonaki
Ⓜ Syntagma

Elina Lebessi (5, F3)
Lebessi has a great range of elegant and fun dresses and evening wear in fabulous fabrics, colours and original designs, with matching handbags and accessories. Also stocks a small range of European and Greek designers.
☎ 210 363 1731
✉ Iraklitou 13, Kolonaki
Ⓜ Evangelismos, Syntagma

LAK – Lakis Gavalas (5, F3)
Gavalas has a popular designer-clothing boutique but this store has his own range and brand, with a range of women's and men's daywear and accessories with a hip edge.
☎ 210 628 3260 ✉ Skoufa 10, Kolonaki Ⓜ Syntagma

Me Me Me (6, A2)
This colourful boutique has a range of young and trendy clothing, bijoux and accessories from local designer brands, including Meatpacking District, Bed of Roses, Fairy Tales, Two in A Gondola and Pavlos Kyriakidis.
☎ 210 722 4890
✉ Haritos 19, Kolonaki
Ⓜ Evangelismos

Vraki (5, E2)
This quirky store is as close as you get to a men's lingerie store. Vraki has an extensive range of funky underwear, T-shirt ensembles and casual sportswear on offer. The store's clever gym theme extends to the lockers and showers in the change rooms.
☎ 210 362 7420 ✉ Skoufa 50, Kolonaki Ⓜ Syntagma

Yiorgos Eleftheriades (5, F3)
Trained in costume design, Eleftheriades is known for his edgy alternative classicist, high-design, hand-finished clothes for men and women, using natural fabrics.
☎ 210 361 5278
✉ Pindarou 38, Kolonaki
Ⓜ Evangelismos

International Designers

Carouzos (6, A2)
Stocks a huge range of quality, stylish designs by leading men's and women's labels, including Versace, Ferragamo, Fendi, Zegna and Donna Karan. It also stocks a selection of Prada bags and other big-name accessories.
☎ 210 724 5873
✉ Patriarhou Ioakeim 14, Kolonaki Ⓜ Evangelismos

Central Prince Oliver (5, F3)
A three-floor boutique for men with in-fashion statements from the stars of the international scene, such as Kenzo, Helmut Lang, Etro, Issey Miyake, Paul & Joe, Anna Sui and Yohji Yamamoto.
☎ 210 364 5401
✉ Anagnostopoulou 3, Kolonaki Ⓜ Evangelismos

Luisa (5, F3)
Fashionistas and dreamers will love the A-list of international designers at this super-chic emporium, including, Roberto Cavalli, Gaultier, Missoni and Chloe.
☎ 210 363 5600 ✉ Skoufa 17, Kolonaki Ⓜ Syntagma

Sotris (5, F2)
Three levels showcasing the latest fashion everything, from clothing to accessories by D&G, Miu Miu, Prada and Venetta Bottega, and local success story Angelos Frentzos.
☎ 210 361 0662 ✉ Voukourestiou 41 (cnr Tsakalof), Kolonaki Ⓜ Syntagma

Mainstream Fashion

Artisti Italiani (11, C1)
This local fashion chain offers quality and fashionable takes on classic looks, as well as trendy designs in both men's and women's clothing, for day and evening. Look out for the great sales.
☎ 210 331 3857 ✉ Ermou 22, Syntagma Ⓜ Syntagma

Cop Copine (5, F2)
For a contemporary look with an alternative edge, this French clothing range has some quality, stylish offerings.
☎ 210 362 7205
✉ Anagnostopoulou 26-28, Kolonaki Ⓜ Evangelismos

Epidemic (5, B3)
A funky gallery-like store with designer streetwear, clubwear and loads of accessories with attitude for men and women.
☎ 210 321 1390 ✉ Ag Anargyron 9, Psiri Ⓨ 11am-9pm Mon-Fri, 10am-8pm Sat, 1-8pm Sun Ⓜ Monastiraki

Glou (11, B1)
Smart, affordable menswear, including casual and business suits and shirts, as well as mainstream sportswear and accessories.
☎ 210 322 7575 ✉ Ermou 49, Syntagma Ⓜ Syntagma

Shop (5, B3)
Located in the gritty end of Ermou, this store has two levels full of trendy international designer streetwear brands such as Energie, Carhart and Miss Sixty for the young and young at heart.
☎ 210 321 6694 ✉ Ermou 112a, Psiri Ⓜ Thisio

ZARA (11, B1)
This popular and affordable Spanish export can be pandemonium, especially on Saturdays – it's better to go early or on weekdays. Stocks a wide range of womens- and menswear, accessories and kidswear.
☎ 210 324 9930 ✉ Ermou 47, Syntagma Ⓜ Syntagma

Don't lose your head over the fashions at Sotris

SHOES & LEATHER GOODS

Bournazos (11, C1)
These Greek designs for men and women have gained international recognition for their quality, workmanship and style. Bournazos also has a good range of bags and leather accessories, and stores throughout Athens.
☎ 210 325 5580 ✉ Ermou 15, Syntagma Ⓜ Syntagma

Charalas (11, C1)
This store has a wide selection of quality leather shoes and bags, from the latest fashions to Nine West classics.
☎ 210 325 8100 ✉ Ermou 30, Syntagma Ⓜ Syntagma

Danos (5, F3)
Artful window displays showcase Danos' feminine, individual designs, made in Greece from the finest imported leathers. There is also a select range of international designs.
☎ 210 362 5390 ✉ Filikis Eterias Sq 6, Kolonaki Ⓜ Evangelismos

Danos – a girl can never have enough boots

Fontana (5, D2)
Housed in a grand old arcade full of leather goods and luggage stores, Fontana carries a fine range of leather diaries, wallets, briefcases and accessories, and travel goods.
☎ 210 323 2093 ✉ Stoa Arsakiou 3 (off Panepistimiou), Athens Ⓜ Panepistimio

Kalogirou (5, F3)
Shoe fetishists will love the offerings in colours and styles to blow the imagination and budget, with top international designers and Kologirou's own creations. Avoid the Saturday morning rush by the boutique set.
☎ 210 722 8804 ✉ Patriarhou Ioakeim 4, Kolonaki Ⓜ Evangelismos

CLOTHING & SHOE SIZES

Women's Clothing

Aust/UK	8	10	12	14	16	18
Europe	36	38	40	42	44	46
Japan	5	7	9	11	13	15
USA	6	8	10	12	14	16

Women's Shoes

Aust/USA	5	6	7	8	9	10
Europe	35	36	37	38	39	40
France only	35	36	38	39	40	42
Japan	22	23	24	25	26	27
UK	3½	4½	5½	6½	7½	8½

Men's Clothing

Aust	92	96	100	104	108	112
Europe	46	48	50	52	54	56
Japan	S	M	M		L	
UK/USA	35	36	37	38	39	40

Men's Shirts (Collar Sizes)

Aust/Japan	38	39	40	41	42	43
Europe	38	39	40	41	42	43
UK/USA	15	15½	16	16½	17	17½

Men's Shoes

Aust/UK	7	8	9	10	11	12
Europe	41	42	43	44½	46	47
Japan	26	27	27.5	28	29	30
USA	7½	8½	9½	10½	11½	12½

Measurements approximate only; try before you buy.

STAVROS' SANDALS

He's known as the poet sandalmaker, and septuagenarian Stavros Melissinos' store **Melissinos Art** (5, B3; ☎ 210 321 9247; www.melissinos-poet.com; Agias Theklas 2, Psiri; Ⓜ Monastiraki) is the place to get that pair of traditional ancient Greek leather sandals, now in 32 designs. Son Pantelis is continuing the tradition with his own designs and art.

Kem (6, A2)
Popular Greek brand. A great range of stylish bags for the working woman, in durable modern and classic designs. ☎ 210 721 9230 ✉ Patriarhou Ioakeim 26a, Kolonaki Ⓜ Evangelismos

Prasini (5, F3)
Imelda Marcos would have gone nuts in this shoe heaven, with French, Italian, Spanish and Greek designer footwear for the really well-heeled, indeed. Not to mention the bags. ☎ 210 364 1590 ✉ Tsakalof 7-9, Kolonaki Ⓜ Evangelismos

Shoe (6, A2)
Away from the main boutique drag, this stock store has an interesting range of discounted designer shoes, as well as a selection of bags and clothing. ☎ 210 729 3963 ✉ Ploutarhou 5, Kolonaki Ⓜ Evangelismos

Spiliopoulos (11, A1)
It is usually chaotic, but there are bargains among the overcrowded racks of imported designer seconds and old-season shoes and bags from top brands such as La Spiga and Kate Spade, usually at bargain prices. It also stocks leather jackets, and there's a second **store** (5, B4; Adrianou 50). ☎ 210 322 7590 ✉ Ermou 63 Ⓜ Syntagma

Thiros (5, F3)
An established Greek label with well-priced leather bags in classic and contemporary designs. Everything from tiny evening purses to work and weekend bags. ☎ 210 362 8445 ✉ Pindarou 21 (cnr Skoufa), Kolonaki Ⓜ Syntagma

Vassilis Zoulias Old Athens (5, F3)
An exquisite range of elegant feminine shoes can be found at the boutique store of Greece's Manolo Blahnik. Some of these designs are works of art inspired by '50s and '60s films – particularly loved that pair with the peacock feathers. ☎ 210 361 4762 ✉ Kanari 17, Kolonaki Ⓜ Syntagma

Stavros Melissinos – providing sandals with a smile

JEWELLERY & ACCESSORIES

Alexi Andriotti Accessories (11, B1)
This Greek franchise gives UK rival Accessorize a run for its money, with stores sprouting all over Athens. An extensive range of costume jewellery, bags and accessories to add colour and flair to your wardrobe.
☎ 210 322 5743
🖳 www.andriotti.com
✉ Ermou 55 (cnr Kapnikareas) Ⓜ Syntagma

Apriati (11, C1)
This is a delightful store with original and interesting handmade pieces from Athena Axioti and Themis Bobolas and other local designers, using semi-precious stones and lots of imagination. There is also a second **store** (11, F3; ☎ 210 360 7878; Pindarou 29, Kolonaki).
☎ 210 322 9020 🖳 www .apriati.com ✉ Pendelis 9 (cnr Mitropoleos), Syntagma Ⓜ Syntagma

Archipelagos (11, B3)
Unique pieces made from silver and gold for jewellery lovers with more moderate budgets. There are also interesting ceramics and trinkets, including fine silver bookmarks.
☎ 210 323 1321 ✉ Adrianou 142 (cnr Thespidos), Plaka 🕓 10am-9pm, later in summer Ⓜ Monastiraki

Byzantino (11, B3)
Reputedly one of the best of the myriad stores in Plaka selling gold in ancient and Byzantine motifs; the jewellery here is handcrafted by the owners, which means prices are very competitive.
☎ 210 324 6605
✉ Adrianou 120, Plaka Ⓜ Monastiraki

Elena Votsi (5, F3)
Votsi's original, big and bold designs using exquisite semi-precious stones, sell in New York and London. Her stellar career was boosted when she was chosen to design the new medal for the Olympics.
☎ 210 360 0936 🖳 www .elenavotsi.com ✉ Xanthou 7, Kolonaki Ⓜ Evangelismos

Fanourakis (6, A2)
Delicate pieces of folded gold characterise Fanourakis' bows, insects and other unique creations. The distinctive designs are sheer art, a factor that is also reflected in the prices. There is also a shop at Panagitsas 6, Kifisia.
☎ 210 721 1762
✉ Patriarhou Ioakeim 23, Kolonaki Ⓜ Syntagma

Folli-Follie (11, B1)
A Greek success story, which has gone global since it started in 1986; you're bound to see these stores around Athens. There's a wide range of watches, bijoux jewellery, shawls, silk and leather bags and other accessories.
☎ 210 323 0601 🖳 www .folli-follie.com ✉ Ermou 37, Syntagma Ⓜ Syntagma

Ilias Lalaounis (5, E3)
Lalaounis' exquisitely crafted, original creations are considered to be works of art. His works display new takes on ancient Greek motifs and inspiration from other cultures, biology, nature and mythology. Lalaounis sells in top jewellery houses around the world. There's also a jewellery museum (p30).
☎ 210 361 1371
✉ Panepistimiou 6 (cnr Voukourestiou), Kolonaki Ⓜ Syntagma

One of the creations found at Fanourakis

Even the displays are a work of art at Petai Petai

Ioanna Kokoloupoulou presents her own creations and work from leading local designers.
☎ 210 362 4315
✉ Skoufa 30, Kolonaki
Ⓜ Syntagma

Petridis (6, A2)
This is a gallery-style store that has interesting collections from Marianna Petridis and other contemporary Greek jewellers such as Katerina Anesti and Doretta Tonti. A good choice for elegant, handmade, original designs.
☎ 210 721 7789
✉ Haritos 34, Kolonaki
Ⓜ Evangelismos

Zolotas (5, D3)
Internationally renowned jeweller Zolotas breathes life into ancient Greece with replicas of museum pieces. Since 1972 the company has had the exclusive rights to make exact copies of the real thing.
☎ 210 331 3320
✉ Stadiou 9, Syntagma
Ⓜ Syntagma

Mad Hat (5, F3)
Brimming with colour and character, this Greek brand has headwear of every style and finish, from casual straw beach hats to imaginative felt creations, along with bags, belts and accessories also sold in select stores around town.

☎ 210 338 7343
✉ Skoufa 23, Kolonaki
Ⓜ Syntagma

Petai Petai (5, F2)
Small individual cabinets contain an eclectic collection of designs, from casual silver pieces to handcrafted gold with precious stones. Owner

JEWELS IN ATHENA'S GOWN

The exquisite ancient jewellery in the city's museums is testament to the 3000-year-old tradition of Greek jewellery making. The quality of workmanship and the competition that comes from having thousands of gold- and silversmiths makes handcrafted gold and silver Greek jewellery a great buy.

As well as traditional designs, you'll find contemporary jewellery by the new generation of artisans in one of Greece's most thriving and creative industries.

The big names in Greek jewellery, Lalaounis (p59) and Zolotas (above), sell worldwide, while new generation jewellers such as Elena Votsi (p59), who designed the new Olympic medal, are also making their mark. Lalaounis' jewellery museum (p30) is worth a visit.

ART & ANTIQUES

Antiqua (5, E4)
Serious Greek and European antiques from the 15th to 19th centuries, with a good selection of silverware, clocks, paintings, icons and 1st-edition prints of 19th-century Athens.
☎ 210 323 2220
✉ Amalias 2-4, Syntagma
Ⓜ Syntagma

Antiquarius (6, A3)
A well-established specialist in imported antiques and collectables, mostly from the UK and France, including books, prints, silver, crystal, embroideries and small furniture pieces.
☎ 210 729 4928
✉ Loukianou 5, Kolonaki
Ⓜ Evangelismos

Astrolavos Art Life (6, A3)
Trendy art shop with sculptures and fun art pieces by local artists that are small enough to take home. Downstairs there are bigger paintings and works of art by well-known contemporary Greek and Greek American artists; there is an exhibition space on the ground level.
☎ 210 722 1200 🖥 www.astrolavos.gr ✉ Irodotou 11, Kolonaki Ⓜ Evangelismos

Dexippos Art Gallery (11, A1)
It's sometimes hard to sort the wheat from the chaff in the myriad tourist shops in Athens, but most of the pieces here are commissioned from a group of skilled artists producing museum copies and original designs influenced by ancient Greece, including sculptures, frescoes, paintings and ceramics.
☎ 210 324 7688
✉ Dexippou 1 (cnr Panos), Plaka Ⓜ Monastiraki

Martinos (11, A1)
This Plaka landmark opened in 1890 and still has a great selection of Greek and European antiques, including painted dowry chests, icons, coins, glassware, porcelain and furniture.
☎ 210 321 2414 🖥 www.martinosart.gr ✉ Pandrosou 50, Monastiraki
Ⓜ Monastiraki

Michael Mihalakos (5, E3)
A good place to hunt for collectables such as china, prints, paintings, glassware, silver, fancy light fittings and bigger furniture items.
☎ 210 362 6182
✉ Solonos 32, Kolonaki
Ⓜ Syntagma

Moraitis Gallery (11, B3)
Takis Moraitis lives and works in his studio-gallery, where you will find his trademark island landscapes and, often, the artist and his students at work. At the time of writing a café was in the works in the great lower-level gallery, with a huge fireplace.
☎ 210 322 5208
✉ Adrianou 129, Plaka
🕙 11am-11pm Ⓜ Akropoli

Skoufa Gallery (5, F3)
As well as regular exhibitions from local artists, the Skoufa Gallery has sculptures, paintings, prints and a select collection of small antique pieces and interesting *objets d'art* on offer.
☎ 210 360 3541 ✉ Skoufa 4, Kolonaki Ⓜ Evangelismos

Zoumboulakis Gallery (5, E3)
This gallery stocks an excellent range of limited edition prints and posters by leading Greek artists, including Tsarouhis, Mytara and Fassianos. Zoumboulakis also sells art and antiques at the **Kolonaki store** (6, A2; Haritos 26) for top-end collectors.
☎ 210 363 4454
✉ Kriezotou 7, Syntagma
Ⓜ Syntagma

The medley of exquisite antique clutter that is Antiquarius

CRAFTS, GIFTS & SOUVENIRS

Aidini (11, C2)
Errikos Aidini is an artisan with metal, with work in leading galleries. You may catch him at his craft in his workshop at the back of this store. Well-priced original creations include small mirrors, candlesticks, boats, planes and his signature bronze daisies.
☎ 210 323 4591 ✉ Nikis 32, Plaka Ⓜ Syntagma

Amorgos (11, C2)
A charming store crammed with authentic Greek folk art, trinkets, ceramics, embroideries and collectables, plus wood-carved furniture and items made by owner Kostas Kaitatzis, whose wife Rena runs the store.
☎ 210 324 3836 ✉ Kodrou 3, Plaka ◷ 11am-3pm & 6-8pm Mon-Fri Ⓜ Syntagma

Centre of Hellenic Tradition (11, A1)
Upstairs in this arcade are great examples of traditional ceramics, sculptures, woodcarvings, paintings and folk art from prominent Greek

Olive Wood specialises in…you guessed it

artists. The cute café-ouzeri has Acropolis views, and there's also a gallery upstairs.
☎ 210 321 3023 ✉ Pandrosou 36 (or Mitropoleos 59), Monastiraki ◷ 9am-8pm, winter 9am-7pm Ⓜ Monastiraki

Georgiadis (5, B2)
A traditional store in the busy Athens Central Market area selling classic Greek tin kitchen accessories,

from brightly coloured wine decanters to stainless steel olive oil pourers, trays, lanterns and even intricate wire mousetraps.
☎ 210 321 2193 ✉ Sofokleous 35, Omonia ◷ 7am-3pm Mon-Sat Ⓜ Omonia

Koukos (11, C2)
This store has a wonderful collection of Italian pewter picture frames, platters,

MUSEUM STORES

Most of Athens' major museums now have excellent gift stores, with exclusive copies of ancient Greek artefacts. Some of the best replicas, jewellery, prints and books can be found at the Benaki Museum gift shop (p19), along with an exquisite collection of icons. The new Benaki Pireos Annexe (p29) has more funky contemporary art pieces and jewellery.

The impressive Museum of Cycladic & Ancient Greek Art gift shop (p21) has exclusive Cycladic figurines and pottery (copied or inspired from the museum's collection) and beautiful books on ancient Greek art.

Athenians just love to shop; Monastiraki Flea Market (p54) is a favourite haunt

jugs, replicas of old monk's hip flasks and other items. Koukos also stocks a range of antique ceramics and original silver handcrafted jewellery.

☎ 210 322 2740
✉ Navarhou Nikodimou 21, Plaka Ⓜ Syntagma

Mythos (11, C2)
This narrow store at the fringes of Plaka's tourist drag has a fine selection of interesting and reasonably priced jewellery, artwork, crafts and other goodies that make great small gifts. Worth a peek.

☎ 210 324 9160
✉ Kydathineon 6, Plaka
🕐 10am-10.30pm, winter 10am-9pm Ⓜ Syntagma

Oikotexnia (11, C2)
Traditional folk art and crafts from all over Greece, including stunning hand-woven carpets, kilims, flokati rugs, tapestries,

hand-embroidered table-cloths and cushion covers. It's run by the Institute of Social Protection and Solidarity.

☎ 210 325 0240
✉ Fillelinon 14, Plaka
Ⓜ Syntagma

Olive Wood (11, B2)
This place has original creations from half a dozen families in Greece who work exclusively with wood from olive trees – a wood that is so hard it can only be carved, not nailed. The shop has pretty much everything, from ornaments to wooden spoons, key rings and chopping blocks.

☎ 210 321 6145
✉ Mnisikleous 8, Plaka
Ⓜ Syntagma

Society for the Education of Greek Women (11, C1)
Set up under Queen Olga's patronage in 1872, this organisation at one time had workshops around Greece and had trained 12,000 women in traditional handicrafts. It still produces exquisite handmade embroideries and weaving and has the exclusive license to reproduce designs in the Benaki Museums.

☎ 210 323 9693
✉ Kolokotroni 3 (in arcade), Syntagma Ⓜ Syntagma

GOLDEN BOOTHS
The *periptero,* the ubiquitous small yellow kiosk, is a quintessentially Greek institution and the best place to call for anything from directions, cigarettes, bus tickets and newspapers to condoms and light bulbs. The ones around Syntagma and Omonia are open 24 hours.

MUSIC & BOOKS

Compendium (11, C2)
A good selection of new and used books, with popular and quality literature, travel guides, books on Greece and academic publications.
☎ 210 322 1248 ✉ Navarhou Nikodemou 5 (cnr Nikis), Plaka Ⓜ Syntagma

Eleftheroudakis (5, D3)
A seven-storey bibliophile's paradise with the widest selection of books from and on Greece, plus English-language books, including maps and travel guides and a top-floor café. There's also a **branch** (11, C2; Nikis 20) in Plaka.
☎ 210 331 4180 ✉ Panepistimiou 17, Syntagma ⏱ 9am-9pm Mon-Fri, 9am-3pm Sat Ⓜ Syntagma, Panepistimio

Metropolis (5, C1)
A music haven well stocked with mainstream local and international CDs. A bigger Greek selection is in the dedicated store further along Panepistimiou.

Anything you care to read at Eleftheroudakis

☎ 210 383 0804 ✉ Panepistimiou 64, Omonia ⏱ 9am-9pm Mon-Fri, 9am-6pm Sat Ⓜ Omonia

Music Center (4, C2)
Across the road from the Athens Polytechnio, you'll find one of the most comprehensive ranges of soundtracks in Europe, a broad selection of music across all genres, and DVDs and Greek movies.
☎ 210 522 4916 ✉ Patision 41, Polytechnio ⏱ 9am-9pm Mon-Fri, 9am-4pm Sat Ⓜ Omonia

Music Corner (5, D1)
An extensive selection of *laika* (popular music) and *rebetika* (Greek version of the blues) are included in the Greek section, as well as Turkish and Eastern music. The helpful staff are knowledgable.
☎ 210 330 4000 ✉ Panepistimiou 56 ⏱ 9am-9pm Mon-Fri, 9am-6pm Sat Ⓜ Omonia

Pandora Music Shop (5, E1)
The place to go for that bouzouki or other beautifully handcrafted traditional Greek instruments, such as the *baglama* (a mini-bouzouki), lutes and tambourines.
☎ 210 361 9924 ✉ Mavromihali 51, Exarhia ⏱ 11am-3pm Mon, Wed & Sat, 11am-2pm & 5.30-8pm Tue, Thu & Fri Ⓜ Panepistimio

Papasotiriou (5, D2)
A major bookstore with a range of travel guides, English fiction and translated Greek literature, as well as photography and coffee-table books on Greece.
☎ 210 325 3232 ✉ Panepistimiou 37 (cnr Korai) ⏱ 9am-9pm Mon-Fri, 9am-6pm Sat Ⓜ Panepistimio

Xylouris (5, D2)
This music trove is run by the widow and son of the Cretan legend Nikos Xylouris. They can guide you through their comprehensive range of traditional Greek music, including select and rare recordings. There's a big world-music section and, of course, plenty of Cretan music. It has a great selection of everyday and collectable *komboloi* (see p67).
☎ 210 322 2711 🖳 www.xylouris.gr ✉ Panepistimiou 39 (in arcade) Ⓜ Panepistimio

FOOD & DRINK

Aristokratikon (11, C1)
Chocaholics will be delighted by the dazzling array of freshly handmade chocolates at this tiny store renowned for using the finest ingredients in Greece. If you're in need of a choccie while in Kifisia, there's another **store** (3, B1; ☎ 210 801 6533; Argyropoulou 8) there. Not one for the weak-willed. Try the pistachio clusters.
☎ 210 322 0546
✉ Karageorgi Servias 9, Syntagma Ⓜ Syntagma

Cellier (5, E3)
A wonderful collection of some of Greece's best wines and liqueurs, with knowledgeable staff to explain the Greek varieties, and winemakers. It sells boxed gift packs. There's another **store** (8, B1; ☎ 210 801 8756; Papadiamanti 10, Kifisia).
☎ 210 361 0040
✉ Kriezotou 1, Syntagma
Ⓜ Syntagma

Fine Wine (11, B3)
A great selection of fine Greek wines and spirits, including gift packs, in a delightful, refurbished old Plaka store. The friendly and knowledgeable owners can

Fine Wine does indeed stock some very fine wine

guide you through Greece's unique grape varieties.
☎ 210 323 0350
✉ Lysikratous 3, Plaka
🕐 10am-10pm Mon-Fri, 10am-8pm Sat Ⓜ Syntagma

Lesvos Shop (5, B3)
You'll find reputedly Athens largest selection of ouzo (29 at last count) at this superb store specialising in traditional products made by the local women's cooperative on the islands of Lesvos and Limnos. There's a wide range of biscuits, sweet fruit preserves (otherwise known as spoon fruits) and other goodies.
☎ 210 321 7395
✉ Athinas 33, Monastiraki
Ⓜ Monastiraki

Mesogaia (11, C3)
Wide range of traditional food products from all over Greece, including cheeses, yogurts and biscuits for immediate

consumption or take-home jars of thyme honey with walnuts, *pasteli* (honey and sesame sweets), olives, olive oil and other products.
☎ 210 322 9146
✉ Nikis 52 (cnr Kydathineon), Plaka 🕐 9am-5pm Mon & Wed, 9am-9pm Tue, Thu & Fri, 9am-4pm Sat, incl in winter only 10am-3pm Sun Ⓜ Syntagma

To Pantopoleion (5, C2)
An expansive store selling traditional food products from all over Greece: from Santorini capers to boutique olive oils and rusks from Crete. There are jars of sweets and goodies for edible souvenirs, a large range of Greek wines and spirits and a fresh deli if you can't wait until you get home.
☎ 210 323 4612 ✉ Sofokleous 1 (cnr Aristidou) Omonia Ⓜ Panepistimio

MYSTIC MASTIC
Since ancient times, the unique medicinal benefits of mastic, the resin from rare mastic trees, have been recognised, particularly the aromatic gum produced only on the island of Chios. It's mostly associated with chewing gum, liqueur, or the sticky white sweet served in a glass of water. A wide range of new Chios mastic products is exploring its many uses.
Mastiha Shop (5, F3; ☎ 210 363 2750; www.mastihashop.com; Panepistimiou 6, Syntagma; 🕐 9am-9pm) sells smartly packaged mastic-based products that make great gifts, including natural skin products, essential oils, food products and pharmaceuticals.
You can also find a sophisticated range of products, including perfumes and candles, at **Mastic Spa** (5, F3; ☎ 210 360 3413; www.unique-mastic.com; Iraklitou 1, Kolonaki).

FOR CHILDREN

Baby Natura (5, F3)
Exquisite clothing and accessories for newborns and young infants, with special christening outfits, bed linen, shoes, toys, nursery decorations and body products – even amulets to guard against the evil eye.
☎ 210 361 5494
✉ Milioni 10, Kolonaki
Ⓜ Syntagma

Crocodilino (11, C1)
The shoe fetish in Greece starts at an early age so the selection of kid's shoes is excellent. The extensive range at Crocodilino is Italian made.
☎ 210 324 4662 ✉ Voulis 24, Syntagma Ⓜ Syntagma

Gelato (11, B1)
Good-quality, fashionable childrenswear for newborns and children up to 12 years old. Most of the clothing is made in Greece and is well priced.
☎ 210 322 1777
✉ Ermou 48, Syntagma
Ⓜ Syntagma

BEWARE THE EVIL EYE

The evil eye is associated with envy. It can be cast, apparently unintentionally, upon someone or something that is praised, coveted or admired (even secretly).

Protection from the evil eye comes from wearing a blue bead or the blue-glass talisman (usually in the shape of an eye) sold in all manner of stores. When complimenting a child (children are considered especially vulnerable), people will pretend to spit on them to deflect any ill effects. Special protective charms (*filakta*), often pinned on cots and prams, are given to children.

Lapin House (11, C1)
This childrenswear store was opened by a group of Greeks nearly 30 years ago and was so successful it now has branches in Canada, Italy and the Middle East. Lapin House offers excellent quality, stylish gear for kids of all ages.
☎ 210 324 1316
✉ Ermou 21, Syntagma
Ⓜ Syntagma

Mauve (5, F2)
A unique boutique with old-world charm, Mauve has a range of *haute couture* baby wear, baptismal outfits, bonnets, bibs and sheet sets

in lace, lush drapes and a superb selection of antique fabrics.
☎ 210 364 0142
✉ Dimokritou 24 (cnr Anagnostopoulou), Kolonaki
☉ closed Aug
Ⓜ Evangelismos, Syntagma

Toys of the World (11, A1)
As well as loads of fluffy toys from your favourite Disney and cartoon characters, this store has Greek board games, European soccer idol dolls and small ancient Greek action figures.
☎ 210 321 3087
✉ Eolou 15, Monastiraki
Ⓜ Monastiraki

Designer boots and shoes for the little people, at Crocodilino

SPECIALIST STORES

Apivita (5, F3)

Apivita's impressive flagship has the full range of its excellent natural beauty and aromatherapy products, from shampoo and sunscreens to its therapeutic honey range. Treat yourself to a 30-minute facial in the express spa downstairs, or you can customise products to your needs in the lab upstairs.

☎ 210 364 0760
🖳 www.apivita.com
✉ Solonos 26, Kolonaki
Ⓜ Syntagma

Ekavi (11, C1)

If you're hooked on the local sport, this place manufactures a huge selection of quality backgammon boards. They also have a great range of chess set pieces depicting the battles of Troy, the Ottomans vs the Byzantines and other interesting theme sets.

☎ 210 323 7740
🖳 www.manopoulos.com
✉ Mitropoleos 36, Plaka
Ⓜ Syntagma

Fair Trade Hellas (11, C2)

It's not made in Greece, but this offshoot of Italy's Altromercato concept, sells products from South America, Asia and Africa that are ecofriendly and against child labour, from companies that provide decent working conditions and benefits to workers. There are gifts, clothing, jewellery, coffee and other organic food products.

☎ 210 361 4070
✉ Nikis 30, Plaka
Ⓜ Syntagma

DON'T WORRY

You see men playing with them and souvenir shops selling cheap plastic versions, but the humble *komboloï* (worry beads) can be a precious commodity, with some collector's items worth thousands of euros. They were traditionally made from amber but you can find them in coral, beads, bone, synthetic resin and other precious materials. Try **Kombologaki** (5, F3; ☎ 210 362 4267; Koumbari 6, Kolonaki) or check out the great selection at Xylouris (p64).

Kamarinos (5, D3)

Kamarinos stocks exquisite antiquarian maps, some of which date back to 1500. It also stocks more than 10,000 faithful reproduction prints from old books and periodicals.

☎ 210 323 0923
✉ Kolokotroni 15a, Syntagma Ⓜ Syntagma

Klaoudatos (4, C2)

Klaoudatos has a wide range of sports and outdoor gear, from leading brand clothing and footwear to camping gear and backpacks. It's close to the Archaeological Museum.

☎ 210 825 6840 🖳 www.klaoudatos.gr ✉ Patision 52 (cnr Metsovou), Mouseio Ⓜ Viktoria

Korres (5, F6)

You can get the full range from local natural beauty product success story Korres at his original pharmacy – at a fraction of the price you'll pay in London or New York. Korres hair and skin care products are also available in pharmacies and at Attica (p54).

☎ 210 756 0600 🖳 www.korres.com ✉ Ivikou 8, Pangrati (near Panathenaic stadium) 🚋 2, 4, 11

Eating

Eating out is a key part of Athenian culture and the city has a thriving restaurant scene. Old-style casual, family-friendly tavernas and grill houses remain popular, while up-scale tavernas serving slicker versions of traditional dishes in stylish surrounds are in vogue. Greeks can do simple wonders with fish and seafood, whether in a rustic taverna or a swanky seafood restaurant. In the city's top restaurants, innovative young chefs are producing sophisticated and creative contemporary Greek cuisine. Renewed interest in Greek food and flavours and an emphasis on diverse regional specialities has broadened the variety of Greek gastronomical experiences on offer.

Beyond Greek food, you can find just about any type of ethnic cuisine in Athens, from Indian and Japanese to pizza and French *haute cuisine.*

Most of the restaurants around Plaka and the Acropolis cater to the tourist market, serving predictable Greek fare. You'll find more contemporary Greek cuisine at restaurants in Kolonaki, Gazi, Psiri and other local neighbourhoods. It's also worth venturing out to the waterfront at Piraeus, south to Glyfada or north to Kifisia.

Athens has a seasonal dining scene, which means many restaurants close for the summer, often moving to sister restaurants on the islands. Alfresco dining is one of the delights of the summer, with people enjoying their meals in delightful courtyards and cool terraces or tables on the pavement. Winter offers an entirely different indoor experience. Many restaurants are also bars, which means they liven up after midnight.

DINING HOURS

Greeks eat late. Lunch is typically at 2pm to 3pm, with restaurants opening around 1pm. Typical dinner bookings are for 10pm and it's not uncommon for tables to start filling at midnight. Some restaurants don't open until 9pm, so if you want atmosphere, don't arrive early.

More tourist-friendly eateries open earlier, but if you want to do as the Athenians do, have a late lunch and sneak in a siesta so you can enjoy things in full swing, especially in summer. Reservations are recommended for upmarket restaurants.

Opening hours for the eateries are based on the standard lunch and dinner hours listed here, unless stated otherwise.

ACROPOLIS & THISIO

Filistron (5, A4)
Mezedopolio €€
A rooftop terrace with Acropolis views makes this a pleasant place for dinner on a summer night; the food won't disappoint either. Offerings include a simple, tasty range of mezedes such as grilled cheese, village-style sausage and meatballs.
☎ 210 346 7554
✉ Apostolou Pavlou 23, Thisio ⏲ lunch Sun, dinner daily, summer lunch & dinner daily Ⓜ Thisio

Kuzina (5, A3)
Modern Greek €€
On the spruced up Adrianou pedestrian street, with tables outside next to the Temple of Hephaestus, and the Acropolis looming above. Kuzina serves creative Greek cuisine, best shared to maximise the experience. The interior

---

GREAT VIEWS

For the ultimate romantic evening with views of the illuminated Acropolis, you can't beat Pil Poul (below), or the informal alternative, Strofi (below). Classy Orizontes (p74) on Lykavittos takes in the whole panorama. For a seaside dinner, head to Istioploikos (p91) in Piraeus, where you can dine (or just have a drink) on a huge boat-turned-restaurant overlooking Mikrolimano harbour. Or take in the city from the rooftop bar of the Grand Bretagne (p98) or the Hilton's Galaxy Bar (p98).

---

design is superb, as is the view from the roof bar.
☎ 210 324 0133
✉ Adrianou 9 ⏲ lunch & dinner Ⓜ Thisio

Pil Poul (5, A4)
Mediterranean/International €€€€
For fine dining, ambience and a million-dollar view, Pil Poul's rooftop terrace is pretty special. This classy 1920s neoclassical mansion has a modern Mediterranean menu with strong French influences. Dress up and book ahead.

☎ 210 342 3665
✉ Apostolou Pavlou 51 (cnr Poulopoulou), Thisio ⏲ dinner Mon-Sat Ⓜ Thisio

Strofi (5, B6)
Taverna €€
This charming old-style taverna has a rooftop terrace with superb Acropolis views and serves a standard array of taverna classics. It was a regular hang-out of the theatre set after performances at the nearby Odeon of Herodes Atticus. Glossy photos on the walls downstairs are testament to its many famous guests.
☎ 210 921 4130
✉ Rovertou Galli 25, Makrigianni ⏲ dinner Mon-Sat Ⓜ Akropoli

To Steki tou Ilia (7, C2)
Taverna/Psistaria €€
One of the best places for meat eaters, Ilia's has celebrity status (and clients). Lamb chops are sold by the kilo and grilled to perfection. For variety, there are pork chops and steaks too, as weU as dips, chips and salads. In summer, there are tables outside, in front of the church.
☎ 210 345 8052
✉ Eptahalkou 5, Thisio ⏲ lunch & dinner Sun, dinner Tue-Sat Ⓜ Thisio

It's worth dining at Pil Poul for the view alone

PLAKA & MONASTIRAKI

Café Avyssinia (5, B3)
Music/Mezedopolio €€
In the heart of charmingly grungy Monastiraki Sq, this atmospheric place has excellent mezedes, live music and spontaneous floor shows. Best enjoyed on weekend afternoons for a late lunch.
☎ 210 321 7047 ✉ Plateia Avyssinia, Monastiraki ☽ closed Mon, Sat & Sun nights Ⓜ Monastiraki

Glykis (11, C3)
Mezedopolio €
In a quiet corner of Plaka, this casual place with a shady courtyard is frequented by students and locals. It has a tasty selection of mezedes, including traditional mayirefta such as briam (a vegetable dish in tomato sauce) and cuttlefish in wine.
☎ 210 322 3925 ✉ Angelou Geronta 2, Plaka ☽ 10am-late Ⓜ Syntagma

O Damigos/Bakaliarika (11, B3)
Taverna €
Reputedly the oldest taverna in Plaka, this basement eatery features in many old Greek movies. It's a lively winter place for traditional Greek fare, just mind your step. The house speciality is bakaliaro (salty cod fried in batter), served with lethal garlic dip. Try it.
☎ 210 322 5084 ✉ Kydathineon 41, Plaka ☽ dinner (closed Jun-Aug) Ⓜ Akropoli, Syntagma

Palia Taverna tou Psara (11, B2)
Seafood Taverna €€
One of the older and better tavernas in Plaka, known for its seafood, is in this charming, renovated 1898 house. It has a great atmosphere and a pleasant shaded courtyard.
☎ 210 321 8733 ✉ Erehtheos 16 (cnr Erotokritou), Plaka ☽ 10am-1am Ⓜ Monastiraki ♿

Paradosiako (11, C2)
Taverna €
It might lack ambience, but for great traditional fare try this small and unassuming, no-frills taverna on the periphery of Plaka. Choose from the daily specials, which include fresh and delicious seafood.

Cosy taverna Platanos

☎ 210 321 3121 ✉ Voulis 44a ☽ lunch & dinner Ⓜ Syntagma

Platanos (11, B2)
Taverna €
This age-old taverna with tables under the giant plane tree in the courtyard is popular among Greeks and tourists. It serves delicious home-style fare, such as oven-baked potatoes, lamb fricassee and beef with quince and summer greens.
☎ 210 322 0666 ✉ Diogenous 4, Plaka ☽ lunch & dinner Mon-Sat Ⓜ Monastiraki ♿

SMACK YOUR LIPS AROUND A SOUVLAKI
Greece's most popular snack comes in several forms – the meat on a stick variety, gyros (meat shaved from a vertical rotisserie) or the spicy mince kebab–style variation.

Souvlaki central is found in Monastiraki at the end of Mitropoleos, where a cluster of souvlaki joints, live music and constant crowds provide a festive feel. **Thanasis** (11, A1; ☎ 210 324 4705; Mitropoleos 69; ☽ 8.30am-2.30am) is known for its kebabs on pitta with grilled tomato and onions.

The hole-in-the-wall **Kostas** (11, B2; Adrianou 116, Plaka; ☽ 8am-2.30pm Mon-Fri) is the place for traditional pork skewers in pitta, while **Souvlaki tou Hasapi** (11, C2; Apollonos 3, Plaka; ☽ 8am-4pm Mon-Fri) serves its version with bread.

Night owls can find 24-hour souvlaki at popular **Kavouras** (4, D3; ☎ 210 383 7981; Themistokleous 64, Exarhia).

To Kafeneio (11, B3)
To Kafeneio is a cosy little place with stone walls and exposed timber ceilings. It offers an interesting assortment of mezedes from different regions of Greece, including Cretan cheese pies and aubergine croquettes.
☎ 210 324 6916; Epiharmou 1 (cnr Tripodon) ⏲ lunch & dinner Ⓜ Akropoli

To Kouti (5, B4)
Modern Greek €€€
Some outside tables have an Acropolis view but if you miss out, the food here is adequate consolation. The Greek menus are handwritten in children's books, but plain English versions will help you select from a creative menu, which includes great salads and desserts.
☎ 210 321 3229
✉ Adrianou 23, Thisio
⏲ lunch & dinner Ⓜ Thisio

SYNTAGMA & THE CENTRE

Cibus (5, E5)
Italian/Mediterranean €€€€
It's not just the location in the cool Zappeio Gardens (in the Aigli complex next to the palace) that makes Cibus a great choice for summer or winter. The award-winning restaurant does superb contemporary Italian-style cuisine in an elegant modern setting. The desserts are excellent.
☎ 210 336 9364
✉ Zappeio Gardens, Zappeio
⏲ lunch & dinner
Ⓜ Syntagma

Furin Kazan (11, C2)
Japanese €€
Japanese tourists regularly fill this café-style restaurant before a second shift of late-night Greek diners descend. Quality sushi and sashimi, as well as some delicious noodle and rice dishes.
☎ 210 322 9170
✉ Apollonos 2, Syntagma
⏲ lunch & dinner Mon-Sat
Ⓜ Syntagma

Noodle Bar (11, C2)
Asian €
This small casual eatery has a range of tasty, Westernised Asian-style noodle offerings. There are tables outside on the pavement and it also does takeaway.
☎ 210 331 8585
✉ Apollonos 11, Syntagma
⏲ lunch & dinner Mon-Sat
Ⓜ Syntagma

Tzitzikas & Mermingas (11, C2)
Mezedopolio €€
Following the success of its two suburban restaurants, this bright and cheery modern mezedopolio opened in downtown Athens. There are walls of shelves lined with Greek products, and the great range of delicious and creative mezedes puts a spin on traditional dishes, bringing Greek flavours to the fore.
☎ 210 324 7607
✉ Mitropoleos 12-14, Syntagma ⏲ lunch & dinner
Ⓜ Syntagma

LIGHT ALTERNATIVES
Healthy fast-food is all the rage at **Body Fuel** (11, C1; ☎ 210 325 7772; Stadiou 5, Syntagma; ⏲ 10.30am-7pm Mon-Fri), with fresh salads, sushi, juices and gourmet sandwiches to take away – or there are tables upstairs. For 24/7 service, **Evergreen** (5, D2; ☎ 210 331 1660; Korai 4; ⏲ 24hr) is a great casual place with a variety of fresh salads, interesting sandwiches made to order, and good coffee.

DAYTIME REFUGES
Escape the daytime heat and hubbub by heading to some of Athens' high-rise sanctuaries. At the Benaki Museum (p19), the café overlooking the National Gardens is a great place for lunch, as is the Islamic Art Museum terrace café. It's hard to beat the panoramic views from **It** (☎ 210 323 5812; Plateia Kotzia), the 8th-floor café in Notos Galleries Home (p54). Above the madness of Monastiraki, in the Centre for Hellenic Tradition, is the little ouzeri and café **Orea Ellas** (☎ 210 321 3842; Mitropoleos 59 Arcade; ⏲ 11am-6pm), where you relax looking up at the Acropolis; there's a branch at Pandrosou 36.

GAZI & ROUF

Dirty Ginger (7, B2)
Modern Greek €€€
With tables around the giant palm tree in the colourfully lit courtyard, this 'post-modern taverna' is a summer favourite in Gazi. The speciality is barbecued meat with a more sophisticated touch, while appetisers include excellent tomato fritters. It morphs into a trendy bar as the night goes on.
☎ 210 342 3809
✉ Triptolemou 46, Gazi
☽ dinner May-Oct
Ⓜ Thisio

Kanella (7, B1)
Modern Greek €€
Homemade village-style bread, retro mismatched crockery and brown-paper tablecloths set the tone for this trendy taverna opposite the train line. There's no menu, just daily specials of mayirefta and grills, done with a modern twist. The complimentary mastic submarine sweet at the end adds a nice touch.

DINING LIKE THE ANCIENTS
More than a theme restaurant, **Archeon Gefsis** (4, A2; ☎ 210 523 9661; Kodratou 22, Metaxourgio; ☽ lunch & dinner Mon-Sat) has an innovative menu based on ancient Greek cuisine.

There are some delicious roast meats, served with purées of peas or chickpeas and vegetables. Diners are seated at solid wooden tables, served by waiters in flowing red robes. There are no glasses (the ancients used earthenware cups), and spoons instead of forks. Bookings essential.

☎ 210 347 6320
✉ Konstantinoupoleos 70, Gazi ☽ noon-late Ⓜ Thisio

Mamacas (7, B2)
Traditional Greek €€
Decked out in cool white décor, this Gazi trailblazer was one of the first modern tavernas serving home-style food in a trendy setting. Try the daily specials or staples such as the Mykonian sausage or black-eyed-bean salad. In summer, outdoor seating sprawls across the street to the courtyard. There is also an attached club.

☎ 210 346 4984
✉ Persefonis 41, Gazi
☽ lunch & dinner Mon-Sat
Ⓜ Thisio

Sardelles (7, B2)
Taverna €€
As the name (Sardines) suggests and the novel fish-monger paper tablecloths confirm, this modern fish taverna specialises in sea-food mezedes. It's a friendly place with tables outside, opposite the illuminated gasworks. It has very good service and nice touches such as ice buckets and little pots of basil to take home.
☎ 210 347 8050
✉ Persefonis 15, Gazi
☽ lunch & dinner
Ⓜ Thisio

Skoufias (7, A3)
Taverna €€
This is a delightful taverna serving Cretan-style food and an eclectic selection of regional Greek cooking, including game and unusual dishes like the hearty and tender pork *kotsi* (shank). There are tables across the road, next to the church. Its sister restaurant is in Exarhia.

Mamacas blends traditional taverna with cool chic

☎ 210 341 2252
✉ Vasiliou Tou Megalou
50, Rouf ☽ dinner Mon-Sat
Ⓜ Thisio

Thalatta (7, B2)
International/Seafood €€€
Housed in a classy tastefully restored old neoclassical building, Thalatta specialises in seafood, but has other tasty offerings too. The sea theme extends to the décor. There is a fine wine list, some excellent desserts and a lovely courtyard for alfresco dining.
☎ 210 346 4204
✉ Vitonos 5, Gazi
☽ dinner Mon-Sat
Ⓜ Thisio

Varoulko (7, C2)
Seafood €€€€
With a winning combination of Acropolis views from the terrace and delicious seafood by celebrated Greek chef Lefteris Lazarou, this stylish restaurant is one of the city's major culinary treats. Lazarou's moved to this industrial neighbourhood from Piraeus, where he earned a Michelin rating. Try the delicious black cuttlefish ink soup or his signature monkfish.
☎ 210 522 8400
✉ Pireos 80, Gazi
☽ dinner Mon-Sat
Ⓜ Thisio 🚕 taxi

PSIRI

Avalon (5, A3)
Bar/Restaurant €€
The atmosphere is part-Greek part-medieval, but the mussels are the main attraction, cooked with almost any spice and sauce you can imagine. The pleasant courtyard opens its roof in summer.
☎ 210 331 0572 ✉ Leokoriou 20 (cnr Sarri) ☽ lunch & dinner Sun, dinner Tue-Sat
Ⓜ Monastiraki, Thisio

Hytra (5, B3)
Modern Greek €€€€
Haute cuisine and degustation-style menu from one of Greece's leading chefs, Yiannis Baxevanis. Let the waiters bring on an array of creative tastes, many influenced by flavours from his native Crete. In summer Hytra moves to the Grand Lagonissi resort south of Athens.
☎ 210 331 6767 ✉ Navarhou Apostoli 7, Psiri ☽ dinner Mon-Sat, closed summer
Ⓜ Monastiraki

Kouzina (5, A3)
Modern Greek/Mediterranean €€€
Right next to the Psiri outdoor cinema, this former factory has a warm atmosphere, friendly service and a creative menu. There's an impressive glass floor revealing the cellar, and a rooftop terrace with Acropolis views.
☎ 210 321 5534
✉ Sarri 40 ☽ dinner
Ⓜ Thisio, Monastiraki

Oineas (5, B3)
Modern/Traditional Greek €€
This cheery place on a pedestrian street in Psiri stands out for the walls of kitsch Greek ads and retro paraphernalia. There are some creative dishes on the menu and excellent generous salads, best shared. Try the cheese pie made with *kataifi* ('angel hair' pastry).
☎ 210 321 5614 ✉ Esopou 9, Psiri; ☽ 7pm-2.30am Mon, noon-2.30pm Tue-Sun
Ⓜ Monastiraki

Taverna tou Psiri (5, B3)
Taverna €
One of Psiri's few remaining authentic tavernas, offering a range of tasty mayirefta. It's cheap and cheerful, with quirky murals and interesting old pictures on the walls to amuse you between courses. There's courtyard dining in summer.
☎ 210 321 4923
✉ Aischilou 12
☽ 10am-2am
Ⓜ Monastiraki

TAVERNA VS MEZEDOPOLIO

A taverna is more casual and far cheaper than a restaurant *(estiatorio),* serving traditional Greek fare and often only house wine. Modern tavernas have a fancier version of traditional dishes in a trendy setting. A *psistaria* specialises in grilled meats, with some basic salads and starters. Mezedopolia serve a variety of mezedes (appetiser-sized dishes, bigger than tapas), usually shared. An ouzeri is similar to a mezedopolio, but traditionally ouzo is usually drunk to rinse the palate between tastes; an ouzomezedopolio is a cross between an ouzeri and a mezedopolio. Mayirio serve casserole-style or oven-baked dishes called mayirefta.

KOLONAKI

Filippou (6, A2)
Taverna €€
Bookings are recommended at this classic taverna in the Dexameni district, which is always packed with locals enjoying the renowned home-style fare. There's a courtyard and tables on the pavement across the road.
☎ 210 721 6390
✉ Xenokratous 19, Kolonaki
🕑 lunch & dinner, closed Sat night & Sun Ⓜ Evangelismos

Il Postino (5, E2)
Italian €€
Small Italian eatery with Italian newspapers for wallpaper, travel posters and postal theme; a popular and casual local haunt. Has decent Italian fare with big serves.
☎ 210 364 1414 ✉ Griveon 3, Kolonaki 🕑 lunch & dinner Ⓜ Syntagma

Oikeio (6, A2)
Modern Taverna €€
With excellent home-style cooking, this modern taverna lives up to its name (homey). It's cosy on the inside and the tables on the pavement allow you to people-watch without the normal Kolonaki bill. There are traditional dishes as well as pastas and salads but try the mayirefta specials like the excellent stuffed zucchini.

☎ 210 725 9216
✉ Ploutarhou 15 🕑 lunch & dinner Ⓜ Evangelismos

Orizontes (6, A2)
Modern Mediterranean €€€€
You can't get any higher than this elegant upmarket restaurant on the hill, with panoramic views of Athens. The cuisine is Greek-influenced Mediterranean, with an emphasis on seafood. By all accounts it's world class.
☎ 210 722 7065
✉ Lykavittos Hill 🕑 lunch & dinner 🚠 taxi to funicular

Papadakis (5, F2)
Seafood/Mediterranean €€€
Up in the foothills of Lykavittos, this understatedly chic restaurant is an offshoot of the owner's successful restaurant on Paros. Seafood is the speciality, with creative dishes such as the stewed octopus with honey and sweet wine, the delicious *salatouri* (fish salad) with small fish, and sea salad (type of green seaweed/sea asparagus). Try the mastic cream dessert with pistachios.
☎ 210 360 8621 ✉ Fokilidou 15 🕑 lunch & dinner Mon-Sat Ⓜ Evangelismos

Prytaneion (5, F3)
Italian/International €€€
This chic restaurant-bar in Kolonaki's busiest pedestrian

People-watching paradise at Prytaneion

thoroughfare has an inviting menu of pasta, seafood and steak dishes and a good wine selection. Sit outside for the free fashion parade. Also on Kefalari Sq, Kifisia.
☎ 210 364 3353
✉ Milioni 7 🕑 lunch & dinner Ⓜ Syntagma

To Ouzadiko (6, A2)
Mezedopolio €€
Tucked away in the basement of the Lemos Centre, To Ouzadiko offers refined, traditional meze dishes and seasonal specials in a cosy setting. There are tables outside in summer. As the name suggests, there is also an extensive selection of ouzo. Bookings advisable.
☎ 210 729 5484
✉ Karneadou 25-29
🕑 lunch & dinner Tue-Sat
Ⓜ Evangelismos

DO YOU WANT SMOKE WITH THAT?

Greeks are amongst the biggest smokers in Europe and the introduction of strict anti-smoking measures has not been met with much enthusiasm (let alone compliance or enforcement).

In theory smoking is banned in taxis, and public buildings and restaurants should have nonsmoking areas – though if you find one it's normally given the worst location. In restaurants people often smoke right up to and even during a meal – thankfully, many months of alfresco dining make it easier to bear.

EXARHIA

Agrafa (4, D3)
Taverna €

Strictly for meat lovers, this no-frills time warp–type taverna specialises in virtually every variation of charcoal-grilled meats, including goat chops, sausages and the offal delicacy *kokoretsi*, accompanied by salads and hand-cut chips. The meat is from the owner's village in Karditsa, as is the excellent red wine.
☎ 210 380 3144
✉ Valtetsiou 50-52 (cnr Benaki) 🕒 lunch & dinner
Ⓜ Omonia

Barbagiannis (4, D3)
Taverna €

An Exarhia institution, this place is popular with students and those wanting a cheap, hearty meal in a no-frills traditional mayirio. There's a variety of big trays of simple Greek fare on offer, such as pastitsio or casseroles, washed down with cheap wine and loads of atmosphere.
☎ 210 330 0185 ✉ Benaki 94, Exarhia 🕒 lunch & dinner
Ⓜ Omonia 🚻

VEGETARIAN DELIGHTS

Athens has few strictly vegetarian dining options, but most Greek tavernas will have plenty of salads and greens on the menu and Greek cuisine is big on tasty vegetable dishes and legumes.

Eden Vegetarian Restaurant (11, B2; ☎ 210 324 8858; www.edenveg.gr; Lyssiou 12, Plaka; 🕒 lunch & dinner Wed-Mon) is the oldest and only dedicated vegetarian restaurant, offering tasty vegetarian versions of moussaka and other Greek favourites.

At the casual eatery **Biodiasosi** (5, C1; ☎ 210 321 0966; Panepistimiou 57-58, Omonia; 🕒 9am-9.30pm Mon-Sat, 9am-3pm Sun) you'll find trays of mayirefta, fresh juices, salads, wholesome cakes and even soy souvlakis.

Efemero (4, D2)
Taverna €

This traditional taverna in an old Exarhia house has been going strong for more than 20 years, serving decent traditional fare with an emphasis on mezedes and grills. There is a courtyard in summer, but it's more of a winter place, with live music on weekends. The occasionally slow service is part of the atmosphere.
☎ 210 384 1848
✉ Themistokleous & Methonis 🕒 dinner Ⓜ Omonia

Taverna Rozalia (4, D3)
Taverna €

An Exarhia classic, Rozalia is a family-run taverna in a huge courtyard garden with special fans that spray water to keep you cool. Excellent-value grilled meats, traditional cooking and a decent house wine ensure it is always lively. In winter you can also go across the street to its sister restaurant, Vergina.
☎ 210 330 2933
✉ Valtetsiou 58, Exarhia
🕒 lunch & dinner
Ⓜ Omonia 🚻

Andreas & Sons Ouzeri (5, D1)
Mezedopolio €€

This is a traditional mezedopolio that is tucked away behind the main street (in the arcade). Andreas & Sons Ouzeri is known for its excellent mezedes (try the octopus or meat balls) and casual atmosphere.
☎ 210 382 1522
✉ Themistokleous 18
🕒 lunch & dinner Mon-Sat
Ⓜ Omonia

Taverna Rozalia's courtyard garden is a breath of fresh air

OMONIA

Aigaion (5, D1)
Sweets €

Since 1826, this basement haunt has served up an endless supply of *loukoumades* (Greek-style doughnuts) served with honey and walnuts. There are also other pastries, including cheese pies and rice pudding.
☎ 210 381 4621 ✉ Panepistimiou 46, Athens
🕒 8am-11pm, closed Sun
Ⓜ Omonia

Athinaikon (5, C1)
Mezedopolio €€

This Athens institution has a wide selection of traditional mezedes and seafood dishes such as fried calamari or rice with mussels. Old-style atmosphere (it's been around since 1932) and friendly service are the key.
☎ 210 383 8485
✉ Themistokleous 2 (cnr Panepistimiou), Omonia
🕒 lunch & dinner Mon-Sat, closed Aug Ⓜ Omonia

What are you waiting for? Dig in at Athinaikon

Diporto Agoras (5, B2)
Taverna €

Go back in time at this quirky taverna near the Athens Central Market. There is no signage, only two doors leading down to a rustic cellar where the few dishes haven't changed in years. Try the chickpeas and grilled fish, washed down with wine from one of the barrels lining the wall. The often erratic service is part of the appeal.
☎ 210 321 1463
✉ Theatrou 1 (cnr Sokratous), Omonia 🕒 8am-6pm Mon-Sat, closed mid-Aug
Ⓜ Omonia

Stoa (5, D1)
Traditional Greek €

This old-style, no-frills mayirio-taverna tucked inconspicuously in a city arcade is sadly a dying breed. There is an extensive menu, but it's hard to go past the daily trays of tasty homestyle dishes such as pastitisio, beans and stuffed zucchinis. It's popular with businessmen and city workers wanting a quick hearty meal.
☎ 210 330 3890
✉ Harilaou Trikoupi 5
🕒 11am-7pm Mon-Sat
Ⓜ Omonia

Telis (5, B2)
Taverna/Grillhouse €

You can't get more basic than this fluoro-lit, bare-walled, paper-tablecloth Athens institution. Telis has been

MEAT MARKET
For a memorable Athens experience after a big night out, venture into the darkened central meat market where the classic fluoro-lit **Taverna Papandreou** (5, C2; ☎ 210 321 4970; Aristogeitonos 1, Monastiraki) turns out huge pots and trays of tasty, traditional dishes, 24 hours a day.

It attracts an eclectic clientele of night owls: from truckies to elegant couples emerging from local clubs and bars in search of a steaming bowl of hangover-busting *patsa* (tripe soup). Exiting at dawn as market traders start hanging meat out is truly surreal. It's also great during the day.

slaving over the flame grill cooking his famous pork chops to perfection since 1978. They come with chips and salad, washed down with house wine or beer.
☎ 210 324 2775
✉ Evripidou 86 ✸ breakfast, lunch & dinner, closed mid-Aug Ⓜ Monastiraki

INNER CITY

Edodi (4, B8)
Modern Greek/International
€€€€
A tantalising 'live' menu, where waiters parade huge platters of the prepared (yet-to-be cooked) dishes of the day, makes for a truly unique dining experience at this stylish, tiny restaurant in an elegant neoclassical building. The food is creative and delicious, with some wicked desserts. For a special night out. Reservations essential.
☎ 210 921 3013
✉ Veikou 80, Koukaki
✸ dinner Mon-Sat, closed Aug Ⓜ Syngrou-Fix

Karavitis (6, A3)
Taverna €
A no-frills, prewar neighbourhood taverna with a pleasant garden courtyard that gets busy in summer and a rustic room filled with old barrels for winter. The wine is drinkable and the food good value and reliable. It has an old-Greece feel and all the taverna favourites: dips, salads, excellent meatballs and grilled meats.
☎ 210 721 5155
✉ Pafsaniou 4 (cnr Arktinou), Pangrati ✸ dinner daily, garden open May-Oct Ⓜ Evangelismos, then walk

DINING TO IMPRESS
For a conventional business lunch, try the classy and quiet Cibus (p71) in the Zappeio Gardens or head to Kolonaki for upmarket meze and great ouzo selection at To Ouzadiko (p74) or the classic taverna setting at Filippou (p74).

If you want to really impress, you can't go wrong with the award-winning Spondi (p77).

Milos (6,B3)
Modern Greek/Mediterranean
€€€€
After making its name in Montreal and New York, Milos set up home in the Hilton to impress Athenians with its fine fish and seafood offerings. The quality is superb and the wine list excellent.
☎ 210 724 4400 ✉ Vas Sofias 48, Hilton ✸ lunch & dinner Ⓜ Evangelismos

Spondi (4, F8)
Modern Greek/Mediterranean
€€€€
This Michelin-rated restaurant in a lovely old Athens mansion has a wonderful ambience and superb summer courtyard. It's one of Greece's finest restaurants, with imaginative French-Mediterranean–style cuisine with some Greek influence. The desserts are exquisite, the service faultless and wine list excellent.
☎ 210 756 4021 ✉ Pyrronos 5 (off Plateia Varnava), Pangrati ✸ dinner ➤ taxi

Therapeftirio (7,B3)
Taverna €
One of a cluster of tavernas in this neighbourhood, this refreshingly simple place has unremarkable décor, and tables outside on the pavement. But the food is delicious, with tasty starters

like octopus in wine and tender calamari grilled to perfection, as well as traditional complimentary halva and fruit desert.
☎ 210 341 2538 ✉ Kallisthenous & Kydantidon 41, Ano Petralona ✸ lunch & dinner Ⓜ Petralona

Trata o Stelios
Taverna €€€
Once the communist stronghold of Athens, the Kaisariani has become associated with the excellent seafood tavernas on the main square. The popular Trata is known for its fresh fish and tasty mezedes. It's a short taxi ride from town (stop here after visiting the nearby monastery; see p34).
☎ 210 729 1533 ✉ Plateia Anagenniseos 7-9, Kaisariani ✸ lunch & dinner ➤ taxi

Vyrinis (4, E7)
Taverna €
Just behind the old Panathenaic stadium, this popular and relaxed neighbourhood taverna has had an impressive face-lift but has maintained its essence and prices. There's a lovely courtyard garden, simple traditional fare and decent house wine.
☎ 210 701 2021
✉ Arhimidous 11, Pangrati
✸ lunch & dinner
🚌 2, 4, 11 to Plateia Plastira

PIRAEUS

Achinos
Modern Greek €€€
Around the corner from Marina Zea, this stylish multilevel place has a great terrace restaurant overlooking the water, with excellent seafood and Mediterranean-Greek menu. There's also a bar below and café on street level
☎ 210 452 6944 ⊠ Akti Themistokleous 51, Piraeus
🕑 lunch & dinner 🚕 taxi

That's a big one Jimmy!

Dourambeis (3, E2)
Taverna €€€
An enduring seafront taverna in Piraeus, this place is popular for fresh fish grilled to perfection and served with a simple oil and lemon dressing, as well as wonderful crayfish soup.
☎ 210 412 2092
⊠ Akti Dilaveri 27, Piraeus
🕑 lunch & dinner 🚕 taxi
Ⓜ Faliro, then walk

Imerovigli
Taverna €€
Opposite Achinos, this modern ouzomezedopolio with cheery seafood-theme décor doesn't have the view, but it does have excellent-value seafood mezedes like grilled sardines. The music can get a bit loud.
☎ 210 451 1256 ⊠ Akti Themistokleous 56, Piraeus
🕑 lunch & dinner 🚕 taxi

Jimmy & the Fish (3, E3)
Seafood/Mediterranean €€€
It's hard to choose between the lobster spaghetti and other seafood pastas that are house specialities, or the daily catch of fresh fish. One of the more stylish restaurants along Mikrolimano harbour, Jimmy's has a great range of entrées, including stuffed calamari, and ouzo and sesame prawns.
☎ 210 412 4417
⊠ Akti Koumoundourou 46, Mikrolimano, Piraeus
🕑 lunch & dinner 🚕 taxi

Margaro (3, A3)
Seafood €
This no-frills Piraeus taverna serves only tasty fried prawns and langoustines, as well as small fish like whitebait and red mullet. Oh,

and potatoes and salad. No credit cards.
☎ 210 451 4226
⊠ Hatzikyriakou 126, Piraeus 🕑 lunch & dinner Mon-Sat, closed Aug 🚕 taxi

Plous Podilatou (3, E3)
Seafood/Mediterranean €€€
The year-round sister restaurant of the pioneering modern Greek Kitrino Podilato offers elegant dining, with an emphasis on seafood, on the picturesque Mikrolimano harbour.
☎ 210 413 7910
⊠ Akti Koumoundourou 42, Piraeus 🕑 dinner 🚕 taxi

Ta Pente Piata (3, A1)
Ouzeri €€
Across from his excellent fish taverna, Tassos Kollias offer a different dining experience with delicious rounds of five plates of seafood mezedes (thus the name) served at €10 a pop. It's tricky to get to so make sure the taxi driver has a street directory.
☎ 210 461 8808
⊠ Plastira 3 & 8, Piraeus (near cnr of Kalokairinou & Dramas) 🕑 lunch daily, dinner Mon-Sat 🚕 taxi

KID'S CUISINE
Not many places in Athens have special children's meals or highchairs but most tavernas are children-friendly, and it is common to see families out into the wee hours of the night.

Of course, the trendier, more upmarket restaurants will probably not be impressed if you arrive with brat pack in tow.

GLYFADA & THE COAST

Bakaliko Ola ta Kala
(9, C2)

Modern Greek €€

This trendy deli restaurant has trays of daily mayirefta specials as well as a range of appetisers, gourmet sandwiches, salads and deli treats.

☎ 210 324 7607

✉ Yannitsopoulou 1 (cnr Kyprou), Glyfada

⏲ lunch & dinner Mon-Sat, 5pm-midnight Sun ⏲ 5

Biftekoupoli-George's Steakhouse (9, B1)

Grillhouse €

Since George's opened in 1951, a row of grillhouses serving *biftekia* (tasty Greek burger-cum-meatballs) followed, earning the area the moniker *biftekoupoli* (burgerland). Great-value grilled meats, salads and appetisers.

☎ 210 8942041

✉ Konstantinoupoleos 4-6, Glyfada ⏲ lunch & dinner ⏲ 5 ⛟ taxi

Kitchen Bar (1, B3)

International/American €€

Overlooking the fancy boats in the Alimo Marina, this trendy American-style bar-restaurant is a relaxed place for lunch and dinner. There's a range of burgers, pastas

FANCY A FRAPPÉ?

Nescafé pulled off the biggest coup in Greece with the invention of the frappé (a frothy version of iced coffee made with this instant brew) that you see people sipping for hours on end. For real coffee, try the *freddo* espresso or cappuccino versions.

and international-style food and the servings are huge. Later in the night it turns into a lively bar. A second branch has a great spot on Marina Zea in Piraeus.

☎ 210 981 2004

✉ Posidonos 3, Kalamaki

⏲ 10am-late ⏲ 5

Zoo (9, B2)

Greek/International €€

This place is in a great location right on the water next to the Glyfada marina. Zoo has an innovative menu with international offerings like sushi and pasta, as well as more traditional Greek dishes with a modern twist. Just ignore the animal statues and sample the generous and tasty mezedes instead.

☎ 210 894 9995

✉ Grigorio12-14, Syntagma

⏲ dinner, closed winter

⏲ 5

NATIONAL SNACK

Since the traditional Greek breakfast is often coffee and cigarettes, by mid-morning the stomach cries out for a snack – hence the *tiropita* (cheese pie), sold in squillions of fast-food outlets and bakeries. For the best, fresh *tiropites* (which come with many other tasty fillings) head to **Ariston** (11, C1; ☎ 210 322 7626; Voulis 10, Syntagma).

KIFISIA/NORTHERN ATHENS

Gefsis me Onomasies Proelefsis (8, B1)
Modern Greek €€€

A stylish, established restaurant located in a renovated mansion, specialising in traditional dishes based on regional ingredients. The food has a sophisticated, modern touch.
☎ 210 800 1402
✉ Kifisias 317, Kifisia
🕐 dinner Mon-Sat
🚕 taxi

Il Salumaio d'Atene
(8, B1)
Modern Italian/Mediterranean €€€

This upscale deli-café-restaurant is an offshoot of the Milan original. There's outdoor seating around a fountain in the shady palm courtyard. The house salad is one of many creative salads on the menu, the mains are excellent and the *crème brûlée* absolutely divine.
☎ 210 623 3934
✉ Panagitsas 3, Kifisia
🕐 Mon-Sat Ⓜ Kifisia

Semiramis (8, C1)
Mediterranean €€€

Even if you can't spend the night, you can still check out

Gefsis me Onomasies Proelefsis...translation: yum

the hotel with the out-there design while dining by the colourful amorphous pool. The food on offer is contemporary and international, with some great salads and pastas and there is a lighter lunch menu.
☎ 210 628 4400
✉ Harilaou Trikoupi 48, Kifisia 🕐 lunch & dinner
Ⓜ Kifisia

Ta Kioupia (8, C1)
Modern/Traditional Greek €€€€

Ta Kioupia is a smorgasbord of Greek cuisine, from the islands to the regions, from modern to classic dishes. The setting is impressive, with great views of Athens from the garden courtyard. There is a set menu, as well as à la carte dining.
☎ 210 620 0005
✉ Plateia Politias, Kifisia
🕐 dinner Mon-Sat, lunch Sun 🚕 taxi

Vardis (8, C1)
Modern French/Mediterranean €€€€

Greece's first Michelin star restaurant, Vardis is one of the big players in Athens' gastronomic scene. Located in the Pentelikon hotel (p98), its contemporary French cuisine and service are exquisite.
☎ 210 628 1660
✉ Deligianni 66, Kefalari
🕐 dinner Mon-Sat 🚕 taxi

Varsos (8, B2)
Patisserie/Café €

A Kifisia landmark, this huge patisserie has been making high-quality traditional Greek sweets and dairy products since 1892. Dine in the old-style café, or sit in the outside courtyard and try the famous rice pudding, honeyed pastries, yogurt or scrumptious cheese pies.
☎ 210 801 3743 ✉ Kassaveti 5, Kifisia 🕐 7am-1am
Ⓜ Kifisia ♿

I'LL DRINK TO THAT!

Good old retsina has its place, but it has unfortunately done a grave disservice to Greek wine, which is finally beginning to raise its head internationally. There are some fine wineries making excellent wines from Greece's unique native grape varieties – reds such as *agiorgitiko* and *xinomavro,* and the whites *asyrtiko, roditis, robola, malagouzia* and *moschofilero.*

The industry is becoming more sophisticated as the new generation of winemakers concentrates on producing the best from Greece's climate and varieties. The results are certainly worth a try (see www.greekwineguide.gr).

Entertainment

If there's one thing the hedonistic Greeks pride themselves on, it's their ability to have a good time. Some years back, the government tried to impose stricter closing times on nightclubs to boost the country's productivity, but a virtual rebellion put a stop to that and Athenians happily party to all hours.

Indeed, everyone from families with children to young clubbers seems to be out at night, which makes Athens one of the liveliest nocturnal European cities.

There's a tremendous range of bars (and *barakia,* the cosier, smaller variety), music venues and clubs, from rock to jazz, Greek pop and folk music. Greek music thrives in all its contemporary and traditional forms, but Athens also hosts rock and jazz festivals and attracts some impressive international touring acts.

Belting out some traditional music

The cultural calendar's highlight is the Athens Festival, which features leading international performers, orchestras, theatre and dance troupes. Athens also has a thriving theatre tradition – ancient, mainstream and experimental – but as performances are mostly in Greek, we have not emphasised theatre here.

Moonlight cinema in Athens' open-air cinemas is a summer highlight.

For clubbers, Athens offers a vibrant dance club scene with top international DJs, and more stamina than most other cities – clubs only start filling after midnight. Most clubs have a door charge and pricey drinks, although the serves are usually doubles.

The Athens entertainment scene is seasonal, so many cosy winter clubs and bars are not open in the summer. The majority chosen here have summer courtyards, tables outside or rooftop bars. Summer clubbing takes place in the impressive big beachside clubs.

FESTIVE ATHENS

For an unforgettable Athens experience, attend a performance at the superb Odeon of Herodes Atticus (p15), one of the world's most historic venues. Set against a floodlit Acropolis, patrons sit under the stars on the worn marble seats (now with cushions) that Athenians have been entertained on for centuries.

The theatre is the main venue for the annual summer-long **Athens Festival**, which brings some of the world's top theatre, music and dance acts. Events are also held at venues around town, from converted schools and factories to former Olympics sports venues.

The **Hellenic Festival box office** (5, D2; ☎ 210 322 1459; www.hellenicfestival .gr; Panepistimiou 39) also takes bookings for the eclectic summer theatre and concert series held at the Lykavittos Theatre (p20).

For information about nonfestival events held at the Odeon in late August to October check out www.cultureguide.gr.

CLASSICAL MUSIC, THEATRE, OPERA & DANCE

Dora Stratou Dance Theatre (4, A7)

Traditional folk dancing shows on Filopappou Hill are a summer tradition. More than 75 musicians and dancers present dances from around Greece in a colourful 90-minute show. Some of the elaborate costumes are museum pieces. If you get really inspired, inquire about its dance workshops.
☎ 210 324 4395, theatre 210 921 4650 ⌨ www.grdance .org ✉ Filopappou Hill
€ €15 🕑 9.30pm Tue-Sat & 8.15pm Sun May-Sep 🚇 15

Greek National Opera (5, D1)

The Greek National Opera (Ethniki Lyriki Skini) season runs from November to June. Performances of ballet and opera are usually held at the Olympia Theatre, Opera House or the Odeon of Herodes Atticus in summer.
☎ 210 360 0180, box office 210 361 2461
⌨ www.nationalopera.gr
✉ Akadimias 59, Athens
€ varies
Ⓜ Panepistimio

Choke back the tears at the National Theatre of Greece (p83)

SPECIAL EVENTS

Epiphany The blessing of the water takes place in Piraeus, where young men dive in to retrieve a cross thrown into the sea. The winner is blessed with good luck for the year; 6 January.

Apokries The Greek Carnivale, when fancy-dress parties are held all over town and revellers run riot in Plaka; February.

Ash Monday At the beginning of Lent, Athenians fly kites on Filopappou Hill, Lykavittos Hill and parks around the city; February/March.

Greek National Day Full military parade in the city along Akadimias every second year (schools parade on alternate years); 25 March.

Easter Night church services, including a candlelit procession on Good Friday and midnight services on Easter Saturday; March/April.

Spring The arrival of spring is celebrated by going to mountains and collecting wildflowers to make wreaths, which are hung in doorways; May.

European Jazz Festival Six-days of jazz at the Technopolis; May/June (see p91).

Athens Festival Music, dance and drama in venues around Athens, the main venue being the Odeon of Herodes Atticus (see p81); June to September.

Rockwave Greece's biggest annual rock music festival featuring top international acts (p91); July.

Synch Electronic Music & Digital Arts Festival At Lavrio (see p91); July.

International Dance Festival At the Technopolis (see p91); July.

Epidavros Festival Ancient Greek drama festival at the ancient Theatre of Epidavros (see p83); July and August.

Full Moon Festival Every August full moon, key archaeological sites such as the Acropolis are open and musical performances held at the Roman Agora and other sites.

Ohi Day Military parade, celebrating the rejection of the Italian ultimatum in 1940; 28 October.

A huge number of operas are performed at Megaron – Athen's Concert Hall

Megaron – Athens Concert Hall (6, B2)

The impressive Megaron is one of Europe's most state-of-the-art concert halls, with superb acoustics and excellent facilities, recently expanded to include an exhibition hall and library. It presents a rich winter programme of operas and concerts featuring world-class international and Greek artists and performers. Programmes and tickets are also available from 10am to 4pm Monday to Friday at Omirou 8. There's an on-site eatery, Allegro.

☎ 210 728 2333-7
🖳 www.megaron.gr
✉ Vas Sofias, Ambelokipi
€ varies; discounts for students & under 18s; book in advance Ⓜ Megaro Moussikis

National Theatre of Greece (5, B1)

This is the country's pre-eminent company, acclaimed for classic ancient Greek tragedies. In summer, performances are held throughout Greece and during the Athens Festival (p82) and the Epidavros Festival (see below). In winter this historic theatre (see p33) plays host to the leading theatre troupes in Greece, though only one annexe has been open during continuing earthquake repair work.

☎ 210 522 3242
🖳 www.n-t.gr ✉ Agiou Konstantinou 22, Omonia
€ varies Ⓜ Omonia

THEATRE CRUISE

The **Epidavros Festival** presents ancient Greek tragedy, comedy and satire at the ancient Theatre of Epidavros, during July and August. Set in lush surrounds two hours south of Athens, the theatre has incredible acoustics – you can hear a pin drop on the stage from the top rows.

The **Musical July** festival is held at the lovely 4th-century-BC Little Theatre of Ancient Epidavros, in the nearby modern seaside village of Epidavros. Performances are held on Friday and Saturday and range from Greek music to classical offerings.

Special **buses** (☎ 210 512 2516; return €17) to Epidavros leave from bus terminal A on Kifissou 100, northwest of Omonia, on Fridays and Saturdays.

An alternative way to see a show is to take a **dinner cruise** (Little Epidavros €55/30, Epidavros €60/35). Coaches leave from Syntagma and Plateia Klafthmonos around 5pm for the Trocadero dock, where a boat takes you to Epidavros. Supper is served on the return leg. Book through the **Hellenic Festival box office** (5, D2; ☎ 210 322 1459; www.hellenicfestival.gr; Panepistimiou 39).

LIVE MUSIC

Most venues have a cover charge (varies depending on artist) and performances normally start at 10pm.

AN Club (4, D3)
Exarhia's basement AN Club hosts lesser-known international bands, as well as some interesting local ensembles.
☎ 210 330 5056
✉ Solomou 13-15, Exarhia;
☽ 9.30pm-late ⓜ Omonia

Bar Guru Bar/Jazz Upstairs (5, B2)
The popular Bar Guru Bar has Thai food coming out of the kitchen downstairs and live jazz upstairs in this intimate space in the grungy square behind the markets.
☎ 210 324 6530
🖥 www.bargurubar.gr
✉ Plateia Theatrou 10
☽ 9pm-late ⓜ Omonia

Café Alavastron (4, F8)
It can feel like there's a band in your lounge room in this intimate, casual world-music bar, which hosts regular appearances by eclectic musicians, including the inspirational Armenian Haig Hazdjian. There are snacks, a lounge area and a great atmosphere.

IN THE DOGHOUSE

The *bouzoukia*, commonly called *skyladika* (doghouses) because of the crooning singers, are a Greek institution, but not everyone's cup of tea. Pricey, smoky and a tad sleazy, with B-grade performers, they are nonetheless packed most nights.

If you are game, try veteran **Remeo+** (5, D6; ☎ 210 923 2648; www.remeoplus.gr; Kaliroïs 4; drinks from €15; ☽ Thu-Sun), and in summer at Ellinikou 1 in Glyfada (☎ 210 894 5345). Be warned, it can be outrageously inflated if you sit at a table, with bottles of whisky sold at exorbitant prices. Not for the faint-hearted.

☎ 210 756 0102 ✉ Damareos 78, Pangrati € varies
☽ 10pm-late Tue-Sat 🍴 4

Gagarin 205 Live Music Space (4, B1)
This spacious live-rock music venue hosts some of the top international touring acts, as well as local groups of various musical persuasions. It also runs DJ events, a cult Greek cinema festival and a music film festival.
☎ 210 8547601
🖥 www.gagarin205.gr
✉ Liossion 205, Thimarakia 24 € varies ☽ from 9.30pm ⓜ Attiki

Half Note Jazz Club (4, D8)
A stylish venue with an international line-up playing classic jazz, folk and oc-

casional Celtic music. It's the original and best venue in Athens for serious jazz. Book a table, or stand at the bar.
☎ 210 921 3310
🖥 www.half-note.gr
✉ Trivonianou 17, Mets
€ €25-30 ☽ from 10.30pm ⓜ Akropoli 🚌 2, 11

House of Art (5, B2)
A well-established live-music theatre, with changing themes and artists from Greek *laika* and *entekna* to Latin, blues, jazz and even poetry and theatrical performances.
☎ 210 321 7678
🖥 www.house-of-art.gr
✉ Sahtouri 4 (cnr Sarri), Psiri € €18
☽ performances start 10.30pm ⓜ Monastiraki

Mike's Irish Bar (6, C1)
This smoky underground pub presents nightly live-rock acts, from local Greek cover bands to international artists. The low cover charge is subsidised by the pricey drinks.
☎ 210 777 6797
🖥 www.mikesirishbar .gr ✉ Sinopis 6, Ambelokipi € €5 ☽ 8pm-late ⓜ Ambelokipi

Greek style Chupa Chups? Interior of Bar Guru Bar

GREEK MUSIC

The bouzouki may be the first thing that comes to mind when you think of Greek music but these days you can hear Greek clubbing music, pop, heavy metal, rap and even country and western.

Athens has a thriving live-music scene for traditional *laika* (popular music), *rebetika* (Greek equivalent of the blues) and modern *entekna* ('artistic' or quality music). Pop and dance hits with a disco-*tsifteteli* beat are popular – and the *bouzoukia* (nightclub where the bouzouki is played) is going strong. Most live-music venues have a door charge; most *rebetika* clubs, including most of those listed here, don't.

Dancers strut their stuff to salsa at Palenque

Palenque (6, C1)
A slice of Havana in Athens. Regular live music, with artists from around the world, salsa parties and flamenco shows. You can take tango lessons earlier in the evenings. The best margaritas in town.
☎ 210 775 2360 🖳 www .palenque.gr ✉ Farandaton 41, Ambelokipi € €10 🕒 9.30-late Ⓜ Ambelokipi 🚍 8, 13

Small Music Theatre (4, C7)
This small venue hosts an interesting assortment of avant-garde bands and experimental music, including rock, jazz and electronic music.
☎ 210 924 5644 🖳 www .smallmusictheatre.gr ✉ Veïkou 33, Koukaki 🕒 from 9pm, performances from 10pm Ⓜ Syngrou-Fix

Kavouras (4, D3)
Above Exarhia's famous souvlaki joint. Lively club with a decent line-up of musicians who play *rebetika* until dawn. No cover charge after 1am.
☎ 210 381 0202 ✉ Themistokleous 64, Exarhia 🕒 11pm-late, closed Aug Ⓜ Omonia

SHOW TIME

You really have to be in Athens between October and April to see Greece's best contemporary artists perform. In summer most big acts go on international tours or work the regional festival circuit, though you may catch some at Athens festivals.

Some big names in Greek music include Haris Alexiou, Eleftheria Arvanitaki, George Dalaras, Dimitra Galani, Alkinoos Ioannides, Alkistis Protopsalti and Savina Yannatou.

Apart from more recent stars bred from TV reality show, the big pop acts are Eurovision winner Elena Paparizou, Anna Vissi, Despina Vandi, Notis Sfakianakis, Ploutarhos and Mihalis Hatziyiannis.

Shows start late and are held in modern cabaret-style venues, where you can sit at tables or the bar, rather than in a stiff concert setting. Ask around for the best shows in town.

Hands up and tags out: it's party time at Rebetiki Istoria

Mnisikleous (11, A2)

A classic Plaka taverna, popular for its live music (Thursday to Sunday). It has a full-sized stage and dance floor and gets very lively. A good place for traditional music and dancing if you can't face a nightclub or *rebetika* club. In summer, there's more sedate live music on the terrace.

☎ 210 322 5558
✉ Mnisikleous 22 (cnr Lyssiou), Plaka ☷ 9pm-late Sun-Thu, 10.30pm-late Fri & Sat Ⓜ Monastiraki

Mousikes Skies (4, F7)

An intimate venue run by a charming singer-bouzouki player couple with a programme of *laika, entekna* and *rebetika* music and an arty crowd. It also serves mezedes.

☎ 210 756 1465
✉ Athanasias 4, Pangrati
☷ 8pm-late, closed Aug
🚌 2, 4, 11

Perivoli Tou Ouranou (11, C3)

A favourite Plaka music haunt in a rustic old-style venue where you can have dinner and listen to authentic *laika* and *rebetika* by leading exponents.

☎ 210 323 5517
✉ Lysikratous 19, Plaka
☷ 9pm-late Thu-Sun
Ⓜ Akropoli, Syntagma

Rebetiki Istoria (4, F2)

This is one of the older *rebetika* haunts, with an authentic grungy, smoky atmosphere, dedicated regulars and a wall of old photos of *rebetika* musicians. It's casual, relaxed and affordable, and thus popular with students.

☎ 210 642 4937
✉ Ippokratous 181, Exarhia
☷ 11pm-late 🚕 taxi

Stoa Athanaton (5, C2)

Located in the middle of Athens Market, this classic *rebetika* club has been around since 1930. It is open day and night and is always lively, with veteran *rebetes* (exponents of *rebetika*) and loyal patrons. There's decent food, too.

☎ 210 321 4362
✉ Sofokleous 19, Athens Central Market, Omonia
☷ 3-7.30pm & 11pm-late Mon-Sat Ⓜ Omonia

SMASHING PLATES

Despite the popular misconception, there is not much plate-smashing to be had in Greece these days. It's certainly not the done thing in restaurants and in the big cabaret-style *bouzoukia* clubs the way to revel and blow your euros is to buy trays of carnations and shower your dancing friends and/or the singers.

At some bars, party animals throw stacks of paper napkins everywhere when the night heats up. Be warned, these acts of merrymaking can be very pricey (you pay for the napkins!).

BARS

Athens has an eclectic mix and disproportionate number of bars, from mellow watering holes to pumping night spots – and everything in between (and often all-in-one). Sometimes it's hard to distinguish between them as many are all-day hang-outs serving coffee and food, then transform into happening bars. In summer, some of the action migrates to Piraeus and the coast, with bars spread along the waterfront from Palio Faliro to Varkiza. Many city bars have terraces, outdoor courtyards or simply spill out on the pavements and alleys. Club-style bars often have a €10-plus door charge, or €10 to €15 after 11pm, which includes your first drink. Bars seem to appear or disappear according to Athenians' faddish nature, so we've selected some classics among the hot new bars in town.

WHAT TO WEAR?

Athenians like to dress up for a night out, especially in the upmarket bars and clubs. Some have strict 'face control', so you may get turned away at the door if you look too casual. Dress to impress.

Tavernas, bars and restaurants are more relaxed but smart-casual wear is recommended.

7 Jokers (11, C1)
This small, friendly bar right in central Athens is a good place for a coffee by day and a quiet drink at night, when the vibe could well step up a few notches.
☎ 210 321 9225 ✉ Voulis 7, Syntagma ⏰ 10am-late Ⓜ Syntagma

Apsenti (7, C3)
Just past the mayhem of the Iraklidon café strip, this casual bar in a neoclassical building is known for its cocktail happy hour, a showcase for friendly Berlin-trained part-owner Dimitri. Best-value cocktails in town on weekdays between 4pm and 9pm.
☎ 210 346 7206 ✉ Iraklidon 10, Thisio ⏰ 10am-late Ⓜ Thisio

Bartessera (5, D3)
Tucked at the end of a narrow arcade off Kolokotroni, with a quirky open courtyard, this friendly place is a cool little oasis by day and a lively bar at night, with a hip 30-something crowd and guest DJs. One space has art displays and it serves salads, snacks and excellent coffee.
☎ 210 322 9805 ✉ Kolokotroni 25, Syntagma ⏰ 11am-late Ⓜ Syntagma

Briki (p88) has the perfect spot in the sun for an afternoon beer

A day could be spent sampling the brews at Craft...hiccup

Bios (7, C2)
More than a café-bar, this multifaceted venue promotes urban culture, new media and the visual arts and is popular with a bohemian, alternative crowd. The café hosts DJ sets and screens arts videos, while performances, exhibitions film screenings and other events are held in various spaces in the former paint factory.

☎ 210 342 5335 🖳 www .bios.gr ✉ Pireos 84, Gazi Ⓜ Thisio, Omonia

Brettos (11, B3)
A Plaka landmark, this quaint little bar has a stunning backlit wall of coloured bottles, old wine barrels along another wall and a refreshingly old-fashioned feel. It's a spirits shop by day and a quiet spot for a nightcap, with a tempting range of homemade brews.

☎ 210 323 2110 ✉ Kydathineon 41, Plaka 🕑 10am-midnight Ⓜ Syntagma

Briki (6, C1)
This tiny bar often gets so busy the crowd spills out on to Plateia Mavili – one of Athens' biggest nighttime drinking holes, where revellers from adjoining bars meet around the fountain. It's one of the most popular low-key and friendly bars in town.

☎ 210 645 2380 ✉ Doryleou 6, Plateia Mavili, Ambelokipi 🕑 midnight-late Ⓜ Ambelokipi

City (6, A2)
A popular spot in the trendy bar strip on the pedestrianised section of Haritos. Most nights there are patrons spilling out on to the road and sitting on the steps of the apartment blocks opposite. It's a little pretentious, but then this is Kolonaki.

☎ 210 722 8910 ✉ Haritos 43, Kolonaki 🕑 10am-late Ⓜ Evangelismos

---

BAR HOPPING: GAZI
Athens' gay-friendly neighbourhood has some of Athens' coolest bars.

Gazaki (7, B2; ☎ 210 346 0901; Triptolemou 31) is a friendly and popular bar with a lively terrace, while across the street **Tapas Bar** (7, B2; ☎ 210 347 1844; Triptolemou 44) attracts a mainstream crowd, serves great tapas and has a pleasant back courtyard.

The popular former kindergarten **Nipiagogio** (7, B2; ☎ 210 345 8534; cnr Kleanthou & Elasidou) has a cute toy theme and fantastic courtyard.

London-inspired **Hoxton** (7, B2; ☎ 210 341 3395; Voutadon 42) has a funky industrial design with clashing leather chesterfields and huge dance floor. Upstairs in **Gazarte** (7, B2; ☎ 210 346 0347; Voutadon 32-34) you'll find a cinema-size screen playing cartoons, great city views, mainstream music and a 30-something crowd. Next door is the rock bar **45 Moires** (7, B2; Iakou 18). **Micraasia Lounge** (7, B2; ☎ 210 346 4851; Konstantinoupoleos 70) has a great lounge bar on the terrace in summer.

Craft (6, C1)

There are few English-style pubs in Greece but at this full-on microbrewery you can sit among the industrial machinery that brews six different beers. Eclectic restaurant; regular tours and tastings.

☎ 210 646 2350
✉ Alexandras 205, Ambelokipi ⏰ 10am-1.30am
Ⓜ Ambelokipi

De Luxe (5, C6)

Funky '60s-airport décor, an innovative menu and an alternative hip, young crowd make this a fun place for a drink or a meal. A great mix of music and a friendly bar team. Dinner's served till 1.30am.

☎ 210 924 3184 ✉ Falirou 15, Makrigianni ⏰ 9pm-late
Ⓜ Akropoli

Galaxy (5, E3)

Not to be mistaken with the Hilton's flashy rooftop Galaxy bar, this tiny place in an obscure arcade is a friendly, old-world place where you sit at the bar and get great service and a little meze snack with each round.

☎ 210 322 7733
✉ Stadiou 10, Syntagma
⏰ 10am-late Ⓜ Syntagma

BAR HOPPING: KOLONAKI

Uphill from Kolonaki square, the bars just keep sprouting on Skoufa street (5, E2) where you can have a quiet drink by day and bop with the cool young Athenians late into the night. The street's veteran all-day bar is **Skoufaki** (5, E2; ☎ 210 364 5888; Skoufa 47-49), a cosy haunt with good coffee and a friendly upbeat evening crowd.

Alu (5, E2; ☎ 210 361 1116; Skoufa & Omirou) has guest DJs playing a mix of jazz, funk and electronica. The three-little-pigs theme and small club downstairs makes **Ta Tria Gourounakia** (5, E2; ☎ 210 360 4400; Skoufa 73) worth a stop, while across the road **Rosebud** (5, E2; ☎ 210 339 2370; cnr Skoufa & Omirou) attracts a casual crowd, as does busy **Tribeca** (5, E2; ☎ 210 362 3541; cnr Skoufa & Omirou) next door. Just off Skoufa, on the pedestrian strip, you'll find the retro lounge-restaurant **Mommy** (5, E1; ☎ 210 361 9682; Delfon 4), a trendy haunt for cool 30-somethings.

Inoteka (5, B3)

Head down the dark alley towards the deserted Monastiraki Flea Market, and amid the antique stalls you will find one of the city's cult bars. This casual, candlelit place gets lively late and at last report was playing some out-there electronica and techno.

☎ 210 324 6446 ✉ Plateia Avyssinias 3, Monastiraki
⏰ 1pm-late Ⓜ Monastiraki

Kinky (5, C3)

This is one of the new breed of small, funky bars hidden in obscure dark side streets in downtown Athens. When we visited, this bar not only had patrons spilling into the alley but also lounging on the ornate bed outside.

☎ 210 321 0355
✉ Avramiotou 6-8, Monastiraki ⏰ 9pm-late
Ⓜ Monastiraki

Discover the 'spirit' of Athens at Brettos

BAR HOPPING: PSIRI

After dark, there's a bar for everyone in the busy streets of Psiri.

The Lilliputian **Thirio** (5, B3; ☎ 210 722 4104; Lepeniotou 1) is a funky, two-level warren of small nooks and lounges, with music ranging from acid jazz to ethnic. **Corto Maltese** (5, B3; Karaiskaki 31) calls itself a swinging bar and it revs up with alternative rock and occasional live music. The atmospheric **Fidelio** (5, B3; ☎ 210 321 2977; Ogygou 2), on the corner of Navarhou Apostoli, has bar stools on the pavement and patrons spilling onto the street. Go Latin at **Cubanita** (5, B3; Karaiskaki 28), which has regular live music, while **Moresko** (5, B2; Stoa Aristofanis) has a more Oriental-Moroccan theme and exotic teas by day.

Magaze (5, B3)

Have a quiet drink at the outside tables on the pedestrian walk, while enjoying views of the Acropolis. Or opt for a more upbeat experience late into the night in the long, narrow all-day bar, which has a large-scale Athens map on one wall and arty décor.

☎ 210 324 3740
✉ Eolou 33 ⏰ 10am-late
Ⓜ Monastiraki

Rock'n'roll (6, A2)

A Kolonaki classic, this upscale club restaurant is rather loud for dinner as it gets very lively. It's known for its Saturday afternoon parties. It's popular with the trendy Kolonaki crowd and has a good vibe. 'Face control' can be strict.

☎ 210 721 7127
✉ Loukianou 6 (cnr Ipsilantou) ⏰ 9pm-2am, closed summer Ⓜ Evangelismos

Soul (5, B2)

This impressive restored neoclassical building has a lively bar, a small club on the second level, an innovative restaurant menu and a great garden courtyard in summer. There's a young arty crowd, good cocktails and a friendly atmosphere.

☎ 210 331 0907
✉ Evripidou 65, Psiri
⏰ 9.30pm-3.30am
Ⓜ Monastiraki

Stavlos (7, C3)

Located in the old royal stables, this is one of the originals in the busy Thisio bar and café strip. There's a great internal courtyard bar and tables on the pavement outside. It is also a popular alternative rock venue that attracts all ages.

☎ 210 346 7206
✉ Iraklidon 10, Thisio
⏰ 10am-4am Ⓜ Thisio

Wunderbar (4, D2)

A trendy lounge bar and café right on busy Exarhia Sq, this is a good place to start if you want to discover this cool, student-bohemian neighbourhood of Athens. There are plenty of casual, cool and moderately priced bars and eateries nearby.

☎ 210 381 8577
✉ Themistokleous 80, Exarhia ⏰ 10am-late
Ⓜ Omonia

Stop horsing around and head to Stavlos for food, drink and music

SUMMER NIGHTSPOTS

Akanthous (9, B3)

One of Athens' more casual beach bar-restaurants, this excellent mezedopolio does a busy dinner trade, while after midnight the bar livens up and is known to turn into a beach party. Popular with 30-somethings, it holds Thursday disco parties.

☎ 210 968 0800
✉ Posidonos 58, Asteras Beach, Glyfada € Fri & Sat €10 ⏱ 10am-late 🚕 5

Akrotiri Lounge

Trendy lounge bar 'club restaurant' in an impressive setting on the beach. It can fit 3500 people and is renowned for huge dance parties, with top international and resident DJs, on weekends.

☎ 210 985 9147
💻 www.akrotirilounge.gr
✉ Vas Georgiou B 5, Agios Kosmas, Kalamaki ⏱ Sun-Thu €10, Fri & Sat €15 ⏱ restaurant 9.30pm-2am, club 11pm-late 🚕 4

Balux (9, A3)

One of the hottest summer clubs in town is set around a pool by the beach with lounges and dreamy canopied beds. It attracts a glam crowd.

☎ 210 894 1620 ✉ Posidonos 58, Glyfada € €15 ⏱ 9pm-late Wed-Sun 🚕 5

Exo (5, E6)

With a great rooftop terrace with views of the Acropolis and Lykavittos Hill, this popular nightspot attracts a hip mixed-age crowd. It is one of the staple drinking holes of an Athenian summer.

☎ 210 923 5818
✉ Markou Mousourou 1, Mets € Sun-Thu €10, Fri & Sat €15 ⏱ 9pm-late
Ⓜ Syntagma, Akropoli

Island

A stunning seaside club, with Cycladic-island décor and an ultra-glam crowd. It's a long way to go to be turned away by the 'face control' – booking for a romantic dinner is your best bet, then stay on as the place hots up.

☎ 210 965 3563/4
✉ Limanakia Vouliagmenis, Varkiza € €13
⏱ midnight-late 🚕 taxi

Istioploikos (3, E3)

This classy bar-restaurant is on a moored restored ship at the western end of Mikrolimano Harbour, and has great panoramic views. The top-deck bar (a café by day) gets lively until late. It's next to the Yacht Club of Greece.

☎ 210 413 4084
✉ Akti Mikrolimanou, Piraeus € Sun-Thu €8, Fri & Sat €10 ⏱ 10am-3.30am 🚕 taxi

Lallabai Lounge (5, E5)

A stylish and cool (literally) bar-restaurant in the middle of the Zappeio Gardens, set among the trees, with lounges, and ever-changing décor. There's mainstream music and a slick glam crowd, as well as a small

SUMMER IN THE CITY

The annual international **Rockwave Festival** (☎ 210 882 0426; www.rockwave festival.gr) and the booking agency **Ticket House** (5, D2; ☎ 210 360 8366; Panepistimiou 42) brings some of the world's top rocks acts. Concerts are held at Terravibe, a huge parkland venue in Malakassa, at the 37th km on the Athens–Lamia Hwy.

City of Athens (☎ 195; www.cityofathens.gr) organises free concerts across the city throughout summer and sponsors the **European Jazz Festival** in May/June and the **International Dance Festival** in July, both held at the Technopolis (p39).

Outdoor summer concerts by Greece's leading artists and international acts can be seen at two stunning venues in former quarries – the **Vyronas Festival** (☎ 210 762 5700; www.ymittos.gr) and the **Petra Festival** (☎ 210 506 5400; Petroupoli) in western Athens. Programmes and tickets are available from Metropolis Music stores on Panepistimiou in Omonia.

The three-day international **Synch Electronic Music & Digital Arts Festival** (☎ 210 628 6287; www.synch.gr) is held in July at the Lavrio Technological and Science Park, on the east coast of Attica. Tickets from Ticket House.

When in Athens…eat, drink and be merry (everyone else is!)

you to this casual all-day bar decked out like a ship (a five-minute walk from the main road). Popular with locals and visiting yachts, it's great for an evening drink and gets livelier late.
☎ 210 988 0282 ✉ Pier 1, Kalamaki Marina, Kalamaki
🕑 10am-late 🚌 5 🚕 taxi

DANCE CLUBS

Club 22 Gazi (7, A2)
One of Athens' liveliest mainstream clubs has moved to a new venue in Gazi. It's renowned for themed music nights and special parties.
☎ 210 345 2220
✉ Dekeleon 26, Gazi
€ Fri/Sat €8/12
🕑 11pm-late Ⓜ Thisio

Envy (5, B3)
The name of this club seems to change every year, but the venue is normally buzz-ing with the latest house, progressive and 'in' tunes of the day.
☎ 210 331 7801 ✉ Agias Eleousis & Kakourgiodikeio, Monastiraki € €10
🕑 9pm-late Wed-Sat Ⓜ Monastiraki

Kalua (5, E3)
A classic mainstream down-town club with the latest dance music (and occasional

but eclectic menu (with an extensive ice-cream selection).
☎ 210 336 9340/1
✉ Aigli, Zappeio Gardens, Syntagma € Sun-Thu €10, Fri & Sat €15 🕑 9pm-late
Ⓜ Syntagma

On the Road (5, E6)
This long and narrow bar restaurant 'on the road' is a patch of green between two busy thoroughfares. It turns into a happening bar at night, with cosy corners and food, and full-on dance areas with guest DJs and the latest club music.

☎ 210 347 8716
✉ Ardittou 1, Mets € Fri & Sat €10 🕑 9pm-late
🚌 2, 4, 11

Pisina (3, D3)
This stylish bar-restaurant set around a pool overlooking Marina Zea is a good choice to cool off with a relaxing drink; during the day you can take a dip in the pool.
☎ 210 451 1324 ✉ Marina Zea, Piraeus 🕑 noon-1am
🚕 taxi

Skipper's
The tall mast at the rear of Kalamaki Marina will lead

ALTERNATIVES

Alternative music fans can find their brand of dark or electro-clash, alternative rock, indie rock, electronica, electro-ebm, even gothic and underground music at a number of venues around town. Here's a few of the leading lights of the alternative scene.
Alleycat (7, A2; ☎ 210 345 4406; Konstantinoupoleo 50, Gazi)
Decadence (4, E2; ☎ 210 882 3544; Voulgaroktonou 69, cnr Pouliherias, Lofos Strefi)
Horostasio (5, C3; ☎ 210 331 4330; Skouleniou 2, Klafthmonos Sq)
Underworld (5, D1; ☎ 210 384 0965; cnr Themistokleous & Gamveta, Omonia)

Greek club music), where there is usually pandemonium until dawn and an under-30s crowd.

☎ 210 360 8304
✉ Amerikis 6, Syntagma
€ Tue-Fri & Sun €12, Sat €15 ⏱ 11pm-late
Ⓜ Syntagma

Memphis (6, B2)
An established tourist-friendly Athenian bar behind the Hilton, Memphis plays mainstream '80s and '90s classics, as well as the latest chart successes. The crowd is generally mixed age, and there are other bars in the strip if it doesn't take your fancy.

☎ 210 722 4104 ✉ Ventiri 5, Hilton ⏱ 9.30pm-late Tue-Sun Ⓜ Evangelismos

Vinilio (9, A1)
The only dedicated 'disco' in town, this place is packed with tourists and locals of all ages wanting an old-fashioned boogie to '60s, '70s and '80s music. It's in the Emmantina Hotel along the coast, and moves to Varkiza in summer (Riba's, 32nd km Sounio).

☎ 210 968 1056
✉ Posidonos 33, Glyfada
€ Sun & Tue-Thu €10, Fri & Sat €15 ⏱ Tue-Sun 🚇 5

Cinema under the stars; Aigli offers the perfect romantic evening

CINEMAS

One of Athens' summer delights is moonlight cinema; watch the latest releases or old classics in cool gardens and rooftop terraces around town. Outdoor cinema is enjoying a revival after surviving the threat from video, air-con and multiplexes. Unlike most European countries, the Greeks don't dub English-language films. Check listings in the English edition of *Kathimerini* (inside the *International Herald Tribune*) or the *Athens News*.

Outdoor Cinemas
The first sessions start at 9pm, followed by an 11pm session.

Aigli (5, E5)
The oldest outdoor cinema (it used to play silent movies) reopened in 2000 at the Zappeio Gardens. It has a deal with the restaurant next door for wine and gourmet snack packs during the film or a dinner-and-movie package.

☎ 210 336 9369
✉ Zappeio Gardens
€ €7.50 Ⓜ Syntagma

Cine Paris (11, C3)
A traditional old rooftop cinema in Plaka with great views of the Acropolis and stereo sound.

☎ 210 322 2071
✉ Kydathineon 22, Plaka
€ €7 Ⓜ Syntagma

PREMIERE NIGHTS

Launched in 1995, the annual **Athens International Film Festival** (☎ 210 606 1413; www.aiff.gr) screens an eclectic selection of international and Greek independent cinema as part of its 'Opening Nights' programme.

Held in mid-September at the historic Apollon and Attikon cinemas (p94), it is organised by movie magazine *Cinema*, in conjunction with the Municipality of Athens.

Cine Psiri (5, A3)
Tucked in among a theatre and restaurant in Psiri is Cine Psiri, a charming outdoor cinema in a rooftop garden terrace.
☎ 210 324 7234 ✉ Sarri 40-44, Psiri € €7 Ⓜ Thisio

Dexameni (6, A2)
Located halfway up to Lykavittos Hill, slick Dexameni has deck chairs, two bars, Dolby SR, table seating and a gorgeous and sweet-smelling wall of bougainvillea.
☎ 210 362 3942 ✉ Plateia Dexameni, Kolonaki € €7 Ⓜ Evangelismos

Thisseion (5, A5)
Across from the Acropolis, this is a lovely old-style cinema with a snack bar and garden setting. Sit towards the back if you want to catch a glimpse of the glowing edifice.
☎ 210 342 0864 ✉ Apostolou Pavlou 7, Thisio € €7 Ⓜ Thisio

Indoor Cinemas
Apollon & Attikon (5, D3)
The beautifully restored Apollon, a historic 1960s theatre, and the Attikon next door have the latest screen-and-sound technology. These two indoor cinemas operate year-round.
☎ 210 323 6811 ✉ Stadiou 19, Syntagma € €8 Ⓜ Panepistimio

GAY BEACHES
The most popular gay beach is **Limanakia**, below the rocky coves of Varkiza, which is part-nudist (as in parts of the beach). Take bus A2 (summer: express E2) from Athens Academy on Panepistimiou or tram A2 to Glyfada, then 115 or 116 to Limanakia B stop.

Asty (5, D2)
A favourite for avant-garde moviegoers, this old theatre has plenty of character and screens art-house movies.
☎ 210 322 1925 ✉ Korai 4, Syntagma € €7 Ⓜ Panepistimio

Petit Palai (6, A3)
The deceptively modern foyer in what looks like a normal apartment block hides a huge, quirky art-house cinema with balcony and old-style bar.
☎ 210 729 1800 ✉ cnr Rizari & Hironos, Pangrati € €7 ☽ closed summer Ⓜ Evangelismos

GAY & LESBIAN ATHENS

The gay scene is gaining momentum and prominence in Athens. A new breed of stylish, gay-friendly clubs has created a busy gay and lesbian scene in Gazi (dubbed Gay-zi), while several more established bars and clubs operate around Makrigianni.

GIRLS NIGHT
Lesbian clubs are rarer in Athens but the casual **So Bar So Food** (7, B2; Persefonis 25, Gazi) is a good starting point. For late night partying, the small club **Onar Estin** (7, B2; cnr Elasidon & Pireos; €7; ☽ midnight-8am) can get very lively. Get the inside info at www.lesbian.gr.

Aleko's Island (5, A3)
One of Athens' oldest and friendliest gay bars has moved to this stylish venue in Psiri. Alekos the artist-owner is behind the bar (some of his works adorn the walls), while partner Jean Pierre plays DJ. Attracts a mixed crowd.
☎ 210 723 9163 ✉ Sarri 41, Psiri ☽ 9.30pm-late Ⓜ Thisio

Blue Train (7, B1)
This casual café and bar, with tables along the railway line, is a popular hang-out on Gazi's gay triangle, with the gay-friendly **Prosopa** restaurant next door, the **Kazarma** club and roof garden upstairs and a number of gay clubs nearby. It's a good introduction to gay Athens.
☎ 210 346 0677 ⌨ www.bluetrain.gr ✉ Konstantinoupoleos 84, Gazi Ⓜ Thisio

Fou Club (7, B2)
This popular gay club plays mostly contemporary Greek dance music and attracts a mixed crowd. It kicks off late.
☎ 210 346 6800 ✉ Keleou 8, Gazi € €7.50 ☽ 11pm-late Ⓜ Thisio

Granazi (5, D6)
This classic old-style gay haunt on the eastern side of Syngrou has been around for more than 20 years. It's a friendly, laid-back place that attracts

a mature crowd and usually plays mainstream music until 1pm, Greek after that.
☎ 210 924 4185
✉ Lembesi 20, Makrigianni
⏰ 11pm-late, closed Tue
Ⓜ Akropoli

Lamda Club (5, D6)
After 2am, this three-level club is one of the busiest in Athens, attracting a diverse crowd. Pop, house and Greek music dominate, with videos in two basement-dark rooms.
☎ 210 942 4202
✉ Lembesi 15, (cnr Syngrou), Makrigianni ⏰ closed Aug
Ⓜ Akropoli

Mayo (7, B2)
A popular and lively bar with a great rooftop terrace overlooking Gazi (and with Acropolis and Lykavittos views). It has a quiet mezzanine-level courtyard and friendly, casual atmosphere.

☎ 210 342 3066
✉ Persefonis 33, Gazi
⏰ 9pm-late Ⓜ Thisio
🚖 taxi

S-Cape (7, B1)
This huge gay dance club has a great summer garden. The music is mainstream but also slips into Greek. It boasts live SMS dating games and Greek-karaoke nights.
☎ 210 341 1003
✉ Mega Alexandrou 139, Gazi € €7.50 ⏰ 11pm-late
Ⓜ Thisio 🚖 taxi

Sodade (7, B1)
This is a progressively funky venue that plays the latest mainstream dance music in the front bar and more progressive house out the back. Sodade gets very busy come evening and attracts a stylish, young, gay-friendly crowd.
☎ 210 346 8657
🖥 www.sodade.gr
✉ Triptolemou 10, Gazi
€ €7.50
⏰ 11pm-late
Ⓜ Thisio
🚖 taxi

SPORTS

The Athens 2004 Olympics left a legacy of world-class sports stadiums. Athens has since begun to attract some major international and European sporting and athletic events. The most popular local sports are football (soccer) and basketball. Visitors who would like to catch some spectator sport are advised to contact the clubs or sporting bodies directly for venue and match information, or alternatively check the English-language press.

The Greek Secretariat for Sport website, www.sport.gov.gr, has information on all sports organisations and stadiums.

Football (Soccer)

Football is the most popular sport in Greece, buoyed even more by the national team's shock 2004 European Championship victory (though its form quickly fizzled and it didn't qualify for 2006 World Cup). There are three Greek teams in the European's Champions league. Greece's top three teams are Panathinaikos, AEK and Olympiakos. Generally, tickets to major games can be bought on the day at the venue itself. Big games take place at the Olympic Stadium in Maroussi and the Karaiskaki stadium in Piraeus (3, E1). Information on Greek soccer and fixtures can be found on the clubs' websites or www.greeksoccer.com.

WORLD'S FIRST MARATHON

The annual **Athens Marathon** is held on the first Sunday in November and finishes at the historic marble Panathenaic Stadium (p39). More than 3000 runners from around the world tackle the 42km event, following the historic route run by Pheidippides in 490 BC from the battlefield at Marathon to Athens to deliver the news of victory against the Persians (he immediately collapsed and died of exhaustion).

Basketball

Greeks are keen basketball fans, even more so after a string of recent successes by the Greek national team, which made it to the final of the 2006 World Basketball championship. Greece won the European championship in 2005 and 1987. Greece fields six teams in the Euro League. The big clubs of Greek basketball are Olympiakos, Panathinaikos and AEK who have all won European titles – Panathinaikos has won three European championships.

The biggest games take place at the **Stadium of Peace & Friendship** (3, F2; ☎ 210 489 3000; Ethnarhou Makariou) in Palio Faliro.

Basketball receives little pre-match publicity in the English-language papers, so you'll need to ask a local or check the website of the Hellenic Basketball Association: www.esake.gr.

Athletics

The annual **Tsiklitiria Athens Grand Prix** athletics event takes place in the summer. Tickets and information are available at www.tsiklitiria.org. The annual Athens Marathon (see the boxed text, above), held in November, attracts thousands of international runners to a course that retraces the steps of the original marathon.

Horse Racing

The new **Markopoulo Olympic Equestrian Centre** (1, C3; ☎ 22990 81000) has provided Athens with a superb racing venue. Race meetings are held on Mondays, Wednesdays and Fridays at 3pm.

The Stadium of Peace & Friendship, a good (or hopeful?) motto for the games played here

Sleeping

Athens has many fine hotels, from grand former palaces and big multinational chains to chic designer hotels and smaller family-run affairs. The city's accommodation underwent a much-needed overhaul in the lead up to the 2004 Olympics. Several new hotels opened and many older hotels were totally reconstructed, significantly improving the quality of the city's accommodation across the price spectrum.

Greece is in the process of changing its patchy hotel rating method to the five-star international system and many hotels have already adopted it. By law, official maximum prices have to be displayed behind the door.

ROOM RATES

These categories are based on high-season rates per night for a standard double room. Hotels have also been judged on location and proximity to the centre, transport and main tourist attractions.

Top End	over €220
Midrange	€100-220
Budget	under €100

Prices vary seasonally and most hotels offer good internet deals.

Athens is a noisy city and Athenians keep late hours, so we've mostly selected hotels in quiet areas, pedestrian precincts or side streets and within walking distance to the metro and major sites.

Most of the top city hotels are around Syntagma, with smaller hotels located around Plaka and the quiet neighbourhoods south of the Acropolis.

Around Monastiraki and Omonia, many of the area's run-down hotels have been upgraded and transformed into boutique hotels. However there is still a general seediness that detracts from the area, especially at night.

The reception of Grand Bretagne (p98) is a picture of opulence

TOP END

Athens Hilton (6, B3)

This 1950s landmark is one of the city's premier hotels. The lavish top-to-bottom redesign is sleek and modern, if a little cold, with lashings of marble and gold, enormous chandeliers and somewhat giddy carpets. It has panoramic views from the top-level Galaxy Bar (and many rooms), a large pool, gym and spa.

☎ 210 728 1000
🖳 www.athens.hilton.com
✉ Vas Sofias 46, Athens
Ⓜ Evangelismos ♿ good
✗ Milos

Electra Palace (11, C2)

Plaka's smartest hotel has been completely refurbished and extended. It has a formal, grand feel throughout, with comfortable, well-appointed rooms. In the front rooms you can have breakfast on your balcony, under the Acropolis. There's an indoor swimming pool and gym.

☎ 210 337 0000
🖳 www.electrahotels.gr
✉ Navarhou Nikodimou 18, Plaka Ⓜ Syntagma ✗

Grand Bretagne (5, E3)

The historic, exclusive Grande Bretagne has always been *the* place to stay in Athens. Oozing with opulence and old-world grandeur, the totally restored former palace wins hands down for history, prestige and location, let

The Athens Hilton is much more impressive on the inside

alone extras like 24-hour butlers, luxury spa and superb views from the rooftop restaurant and bar.

☎ 210 333 0000
🖳 www.grandebretagne.gr
✉ Vas Georgiou 1, Syntagma Sq Ⓜ Syntagma
♿ good ✗ GB Corner, Roof Garden 🛗

King George II Palace (5, E3)

Originally an annexe of the presidential palace, this landmark hotel was a derelict eyesore for 15 years before being totally restored, with all the opulence befitting its history. A member of the Leading Hotels of the World, the decadence extends from the flaming torch entry and marble foyer to the royal penthouse with private pool.

☎ 210 322 2210 🖳 www
.grecotel.gr ✉ Syntagma Sq
Ⓜ Syntagma ♿ excellent
✗ Tudor Hall 🛗

Margi Hotel

An exquisite, boutique hotel where the personal touch of the owners (two sisters) includes antiques, handmade furniture and decorative items collected on their travels. The suites are divine. If you don't need to be in town, the Margi is right next to the beach, with a great pool bar and restaurant.

☎ 210 896 2061
🖳 www.themargi.gr
✉ Litous 11, Vouliagmeni
🚕 taxi ♿ excellent
✗ Cafe Tabac

Pentelikon (8, C1)

One of the most decadent options in Athens, the exclusive Pentelikon is in a neoclassical mansion in leafy Kifisia, and boasts a swimming pool, manicured garden and beautifully furnished rooms. Faultless service, a luxury old-world style and a Michelin-rated restaurant make it a real treat.

☎ 210 623 0650
🖳 www.hotelpentelikon.gr
✉ Deligianni 66, Kefalari
🚕 taxi ✗ Vardis (p80)

BOOK ACCOMMODATION ONLINE

For more recommendations by Lonely Planet authors, check out the online booking service at www.lonely planet.com.

St George Lycabettus (6, A2)

This historic hotel at the foot of pine-clad Lykavittos Hill has great views of the city. There is an impressive art collection and the individually decorated rooms are modern, stylish and well appointed. The suites are lavish. There's a rooftop pool and bar, two restaurants and a luxury spa. The uphill hike is the catch.

☎ 210 729 0711
🖳 www.sglycabettus.gr
✉ Kleomenous 2, Plateia Dexameni, Kolonaki
Ⓜ Evangelismos
✗ Le Grand Balcon

Semiramis Hotel (8, C1)

With its pink-and-lime façade and lollipop colours inside, this 52-room art hotel by renowned industrial designer Karim Rashid is the coolest place to stay if you don't need to be downtown. It boasts contemporary art, an impressive amorphous pool and many fun hi-tech gadgets and features in the rooms.

☎ 210 628 4400
🖳 www.semiramisathens .com ✉ Trikoupi 48, Kifisia Ⓜ Kifisia
✗ Semiramis (p80)

MIDRANGE

Achilleas (11, C1)

From the sleek lobby to the rooms, the Achilleas has been tastefully renovated. Large and airy rooms have TV and fridge, and those on the top floor open onto garden balconies. There are large family rooms. This place is a bargain in winter and has specials online.

☎ 210 322 2707
🖳 www.achilleashotel.gr
✉ Leka 21, Syntagma
Ⓜ Syntagma ⚄

Alexandros (6, C1)

A small luxury hotel popular with business travellers, Alexandros has spacious rooms, excellent facilities and a pleasant, contemporary design. The upper floors have generous balconies with views over the city. Pets can be accommodated.

☎ 210 643 0464 🖳 www .alexandroshotelathens.com ✉ Timoleontos Vassou 8, Plateia Mavili, Ambelokipi
Ⓜ Megaro Moussikis
✗ Don Giovanni

Andromeda (6, C1)

A member of Small Luxury Hotels of the World, this boutique hotel is in a quiet, tree-lined street behind the Athens Concert Hall and the US embassy. Stylish and intimate, it has all the mod cons on a smaller scale. The rooms are small but comfortable and the service excellent, with another 12 executive apartments nearby.

☎ 210 641 5000
🖳 www.andromedaathens .gr ✉ Timoleontos Vassou 22, Ambelokipi Ⓜ Ambelokipi ✗

Arion Hotel (5, B2)

This good value three-star hotel overlooks Agios Dimitriou Sq in Psiri but also enjoys views of the Acropolis from the top rooms and roof garden. The décor is rather bland but the rooms have the necessary mod cons, are tastefully furnished and have marble bathrooms. It is a short walk to Monastiraki station.

☎ 210 324 0417
🖳 www.arion-athens.gr
✉ Agios Dimitriou 18, Psiri
Ⓜ Monastiraki ✗ Taverna tou Psiri (p73)

Athens Cypria Hotel (11, C1)

A small hotel in the heart of town, the Cypria offers excellent value, comfort

Why go up to your room when the couches are so comfy at Alexandros' reception?

and convenience just off the Ermou shopping precinct. Rooms have a minibar and room service. Adjoining family rooms, cribs and discounts for children make this a good family option.

☎ 210 323 8034/8
🖥 www.athenscypria.com
✉ Diomias 5, Syntagma
Ⓜ Syntagma ♿

Central Hotel (11, C2)
This stylish hotel has been tastefully decorated in light, contemporary tones. It has comfortable rooms with all the mod cons and decent bathrooms. There is a lovely roof terrace with Acropolis views, which has a small Jacuzzi and sun lounges. The Central is in a handy location between Syntagma and Plaka.

☎ 210 322 1553
🖥 www.centralhotel.gr
✉ Apollonos 21, Plaka
Ⓜ Syntagma

Fresh Hotel (5, C2)
This hotel with its bright and fresh design led the trend for hip hotels in the gritty Omonia area. Once inside, the seediness gives way to chic rooms and suites with bright colour schemes, clever lighting and all the mod cons. The big surprise here is the rooftop with pool, bar and restaurant with Acropolis views.

☎ 210 524 8511 🖥 www .freshhotel.gr ✉ Sofokleous 26 (cnr Klisthenous), Omonia
Ⓜ Omonia ✖ Air Lounge

Hera Hotel (5, C6)
This elegant boutique hotel was totally rebuilt but the interior design is in keeping with the lovely neoclassical façade. There's lots of brass and timber and stylish classic furnishings, along with all the expected amenities. The rooftop restaurant and bar have spectacular views.

☎ 210 923 6682
🖥 www.herahotel.gr
✉ Falirou 9, Akropoli
Ⓜ Akropoli ✖ Peacock

Herodion (5, C6)
This elegant modern hotel has comfortable rooms and service. There is a lovely atrium restaurant and laptops with high-speed internet connection in the lobby. The roof terrace has two Jacuzzis, sun loungers and Acropolis views.

☎ 210 923 6832/6
🖥 www.herodion.gr
✉ Rovertou Galli 4, Makrigianni Ⓜ Akropoli ✖ ♿

Hotel Adrian (11, A2)
This small hotel is conveniently located off Plateia Arhaia Agoras in the heart of Plaka. Breakfast is on a lovely shady terrace with Acropolis views. The well-equipped rooms have been refurbished and are pleasant enough, but the 3rd-floor rooms are the best, with large balconies overlooking the square.

☎ 210 322 1553
🖥 www.douros-hotels.com
✉ Adrianou 74, Plaka
Ⓜ Monastiraki

Magna Grecia (11, B1)
This historic building on busy Mitropoleos, opposite the cathedral, has great Acropolis views from the front rooms and rooftop terrace. There are 12 individually decorated rooms with painted murals, named after Greek islands. The rooms have Cocomat eco-mattresses and furniture, DVD and internet facilities and minibars.

☎ 210 324 0314
🖥 www.magnagreciahotel .com ✉ Mitropoleos 54
Ⓜ Monastiraki ✖ Tzitzikas & Mermingas (p71)

Niki Hotel (11, C2)
This small hotel bordering Plaka has undergone one of the more stylish makeovers in the area. It has a contem-

St George Lycabettus (p99) – you really can't miss it

porary design and furnishings, well-appointed rooms and there is a two-level suite for families. Some rooms have balconies with Acropolis views.

☎ 210 322 0913
💻 www.nikihotel.gr
✉ Nikis 27, Syntagma
Ⓜ Syntagma

Ochre & Brown (5, A3)

This small, 11-room boutique hotel is one of the new breed of design hotel contenders, with all the mod cons including flat-screen TVs and fancy sheets and pillows. It is conveniently located in the Thisio end of grungy Psiri, near the nightlife and restaurants and all the major sites. There's wireless internet and a bar-restaurant.

☎ 210 331 2950 💻 www
.ochreandbrown.com
✉ Leokoriou 7, Psiri
Ⓜ Thisio ✗

Periscope (6, A2)

Right in chic Kolonaki overlooking Lykavittos, Periscope is a smart, modern hotel with industrial décor and many clever gadgets and design features, including the lobby slide show, the sea level measure on the stairs, travelling TVs and aerial shots of Athens on the ceilings. The penthouse's private rooftop Jacuzzi has sensational views.

☎ 210 729 7200
💻 www.periscope.gr
✉ Haritos 22, Kolonaki
Ⓜ Evangelismos

Philippos Hotel (5, C6)

A great midrange hotel near the Acropolis, Philippos has a good reputation for service and is popular with business

and leisure travellers. The rooms are not as impressively appointed as the public areas but are comfortable and have all you need. A small double room on the roof has a private terrace.

☎ 210 922 3611
💻 www.philipposhotel.gr
✉ Mitseon 3, Makrigianni
Ⓜ Akropoli 🚼

Plaka Hotel (11, B1)

It's hard to beat the Acropolis views from the rooftop garden and top-floor rooms of this refurbished hotel, right on the edge of Plaka. Rooms have light timber furniture and floors, and satellite TV, though the bathrooms are on the small side.

☎ 210 322 2096
💻 www.plakahotel.gr
✉ Kapnikareas 7 (cnr Mitropoleos) Ⓜ Monastiraki

Twenty-One (8, C1)

The art on the walls and lofts with skylights over the bed, where you can sleep under the stars, are one of the many unique and clever design aspects of this new designer hotel in leafy Kifisia. The style is contemporary and it is well equipped with hi-tech gadgets for business travellers.

☎ 210 623 3521 💻 www
.twentyone.gr ✉ Kolokotroni 21 (cnr Mykonou),
Kifisia Ⓜ Kifisia ✗ 21

Acro_____ _, C2)

This atmospheric old pension in a 19th-century Plaka residence is favoured by artists and academics. The family-run hotel has 20 large, basic and clean rooms with original frescoes and simple décor. Some rooms have en suites and others have private bathrooms down the hall. Most have air-con.

☎ 210 322 2344; 💻 www
.acropolishouse.gr ✉ Kodrou 6-8, Plaka Ⓜ Syntagma

Acropolis View (5, B6)

This small, friendly hotel is in a quiet location, just south of the Odeon of Herodes Atticus. There are indeed views of the Acropolis from some of the rooms, although the best vistas are from the roof terrace. Other rooms look out towards Filopappou Hill. The plainly decorated rooms are well-equipped and have new bathrooms.

☎ 210 921 7303 💻 www
.acropolisview.gr ✉ Webster 10 (off Rovertou Galli),
Makrigianni Ⓜ Akropoli

Art Gallery Hotel (4, B7)

This small, family-run and friendly place is full of personal touches and artwork by an artist who once had her studio upstairs. Some

Favoured by artsy types –
Acropolis House (p101)

rooms are small but all have
been refurbished, with new
bathrooms. Original furniture
from the '60s and a balcony
with Acropolis views add to
the hotel's charm.
☎ 210 923 8376
🖳 www.artgalleryhotel.gr
✉ Erehthiou 5, Koukaki
Ⓜ Syngrou-Fix

Athens Studios (5, C6)
Stylish new furnished apartments in a handy location to
Athens' sights, with flexible
sleeping options, making
them ideal for families or
groups and those wanting
longer stays (minimum
three-night stay). There's a
well-equipped kitchen, air-
con, plasma-screen TVs, work
spaces, free ADSL connection
and small balconies.
☎ 210 922 4044 🖳 www
.athensstudios.gr ✉ Veikou
3A, Makrigianni Ⓜ Akropoli

Cecil Hotel (5, C2)
This fine old family-run hotel
is a charming, good-value
place to stay. It has polished
timber floors, decorative
high moulded ceilings and
original cage-style lift. The
36 tastefully furnished rooms
have TV, air-con and minibar.
Soundproofing is planned but
in the meantime get a room
at the back.
☎ 210 321 7079 🖳 www
.cecil.gr ✉ Athinas 39,
Monastiraki Ⓜ Monastiraki

Erechtion (5, A4)
The pedestrian promenade
around Thisio has boosted
the appeal of the area's
budget hotels. This hotel is
slowly refurbishing its rooms,
many of which have great
Acropolis views. They are
clean and all have air-con
and TV, but the bulk of the
rooms are still dated. The
glass cabinet of kitsch in the
foyer sets the tone.
☎ 210 345 9606; fax 210
345 9626 ✉ Flammarion
8, Thisio Ⓜ Thisio
✖ Filistron (p69)

Hotel Exarchion (4, D3)
Right in the heart of bohemian Exarhia, this dated and
rather bland 1960s high-rise
hotel offers cheap and clean
accommodation in one of
Athens most interesting (and
non-touristy) neighbour-
hoods. There are washing
facilities, an internet café in
the foyer and a rooftop café-
bar. It's a 10-minute walk
from Omonia.
☎ 210 380 0731
🖳 www.exarchion.com
✉ Themistokleous 55,
Exarhia Ⓜ Omonia
✖ Taverna Rozalia (p75)

Marble House Pension (4, B8)
This pension in a quiet
cul-de-sac off Zini is one
of Athens' better budget
hotels, though it is a fair
walk from the tourist areas.
Rooms have been updated,
with new pine beds and
linen. All rooms have a
fridge and ceiling fans and
some have air-con.
☎ 210 923 4058 🖳 www
.marble.house.gr ✉ Zini 35,
Koukaki Ⓜ Syngrou-Fix

Student & Travellers' Inn (11, C3)
Along with the budget
dorms, this popular and
well-run place in the heart
of Plaka has simple rooms
for up to four people, that
come with or without
private bathroom and air-
conditioning. It has a cheery
yellow and blue colour
scheme and some rooms
have fine old timber floors.
There's a shady courtyard
with large-screen TV,
internet access and a travel
service.
☎ 210 324 4808 🖳 www
.studenttravellersinn.com
✉ Kydathineon 16, Plaka
Ⓜ Syntagma

Tempi Hotel (11, A1)
Tempi is a friendly, family-
run, no-frills hotel located
on a pleasant pedestrian
strip. The hotel has basic,
clean rooms, and most come
with private bathroom and
satellite TV. There is a com-
munal fridge and tea- and
coffee-making facilities. The
front rooms have balconies
overlooking pretty Plateia
Agia Irini, and views of the
Acropolis. The top-floor
rooms are small and quite
a hike.
☎ 210 321 3175 🖳 www
.tempihotel.gr ✉ Eolou 29,
Athens Ⓜ Monastiraki

About Athens

HISTORY

Ancient Athens

The Acropolis drew some of Greece's earliest Neolithic settlers. By 1400 BC, it had become a powerful Mycenaean city whose territory covered most of Attica. By the end of the 7th century BC, Athens was the artistic centre of Greece.

Not just a pretty face, Hadrian (p104) prettied up Athens too

Athens was ruled by aristocrats and tyrants until Solon, the harbinger of democracy, became *arhon* (chief magistrate) in 594 BC and declared all free Athenians equal by law. He introduced sweeping social and economic reforms that led to Athens becoming the cradle of European civilisation and democracy.

In 490 BC, the Persian army reached Attica but were humiliatingly defeated when outmanoeuvred in the Battle of Marathon. They returned in 480 BC, and virtually burned Athens to the ground.

Classical Age

Under Pericles' leadership (461–429 BC), the treasury moved from Delos to Athens and an illustrious rebuilding programme began. Athens experienced a golden age of unprecedented cultural, artistic and scientific achievement.

However Athens' expansionist ambitions eventually sparked the Peloponnesian Wars, in which Athens suffered badly. During the first war (431–421 BC) a plague broke out, killing a third of the city's population, including Pericles. After Athens surrendered to Sparta in the second war, its fleet was confiscated and the Delian League, the alliance of Greek city-states formed to defend against the Persians, was abolished.

Hellenistic Period

The northern kingdom of Macedon led by Philip II emerged as the new power in 338 BC. After Philip's assassination, his son Alexander (the Great) became king and by the end of the 3rd century BC had spread Hellenism into Persia, Egypt and parts of India and Afghanistan. Alexander treated

ATHENS MYTHOLOGY

The history of Athens is steeped in myths and legends. The goddess Athena became the patron deity of the city after winning a contest with Poseidon. King Kekrops, the founder and first king of Athens, declared that the honour would be given to whoever gave the city the best gift. Athena produced an olive tree, providing oil, food and wood. Poseidon (god of the sea) struck a rock with his trident producing a spring, but it turned out to be salt water. Another version has Poseidon presenting horses. Either way, Athena won.

Athens favourably. His tutor Aristotle taught at the Athens Lyceum. But an unsuccessful bid for independence after Alexander's death led to an intermittent period of subjection to Macedon, although the city's institutions were upheld.

Roman Rule

Athens was defeated by Rome in 189 BC after it backed an enemy of Rome in Asia Minor, but the city escaped lightly as the Romans had great respect for Athenian scholarship and supported the teachings of Athenian philosophers. After a second ill-fated rebellion, the Romans destroyed the city walls and carted off many of its finest statues to Rome.

Athens received a pardon from Julius Caesar and, for the next 300 years, it experienced an unprecedented period of peace – the Pax Romana – and became the seat of learning, attracting the sons of rich Romans. During this period Roman emperors, particularly Hadrian, graced Athens with many grand buildings.

Byzantine Empire

With the rise of the Byzantine Empire, which blended Hellenistic culture with Christianity, the Greek city of Byzantium (renamed Constantinople in AD 330, present-day Istanbul) became the capital of the Roman Empire.

The Byzantine Empire outlived Rome, lasting until the Turks captured Constantinople in 1453. Christianity was made the official religion of Greece in 394, and worship of Greek and Roman gods was banned.

Athens remained an important cultural centre until 529, when the teaching of 'pagan' classical philosophy was forbidden in favour of Christian theology. From 1200 to 1450, Athens was occupied by a succession of opportunistic invaders – Franks, Catalans, Florentines and Venetians.

Ottoman Rule

In 1456 Athens was captured by the Turks, who ruled Greece for the next 400 years. The Acropolis became the home of the Ottoman governor, the Parthenon was converted into a mosque and the Erechtheion was used as a harem. Athens enjoyed a privileged administrative status and

Imposing, no? Fresco in the main building of Athens University (p33)

a period of relative peace ensued, with some economic prosperity from trade, particularly with the Venetians. Conflict between the Turks and Venetians led the Venetian general Morosini to lay siege to the Acropolis for two months in 1687, briefly interrupting Turkish control of the city. During this campaign, the Parthenon was blown up when Venetian artillery struck gunpowder stored inside the temple.

Independence

On 25 March 1821 the Greeks launched the War of Independence and on 13 January 1822 independence was declared. But infighting twice escalated into civil war, allowing the Ottomans to recapture Athens, whereupon the Western powers stepped in and destroyed the Turkish-Egyptian fleet in the Bay of Navarino.

In April 1827 Ioannis Kapodistrias was elected president, and the city of Nafplio was named the capital. After Kapodistrias was assassinated in 1831, Britain, France and Russia again intervened, declaring Greece a monarchy. To avoid taking sides, the throne was given to 17-year-old Prince Otto of Bavaria, who transferred his court to Athens, which became the capital in 1834.

At the time there were about 6000 residents in Athens, many having fled after Athens suffered in the siege of 1827. King Otto (as he became) brought in Bavarian architects to create a city of imposing neoclassical buildings, tree-lined boulevards and squares. Sadly, many of these building have been demolished.

WWII & the Greek Civil War

Athens thrived and enjoyed a brief heyday as the 'Paris of the eastern Mediterranean' before WWI. A disastrous Greek attempt to seize former Greek territories in southern Turkey, known as the Asia Minor catastrophe, ended with the Treaty of Lausanne in July 1923.

More than one million Greeks were forced out of Turkey in the ensuing population exchange. Athens' population virtually doubled overnight.

During the German occupation of WWII, more Athenians were killed by starvation than by the enemy. After the war, fighting between communist and monarchist resistance groups led to a bitter civil war that ended in October 1949, leaving the country in a political, social and economic mess.

In a mass exodus, almost a million Greeks migrated to the USA, Canada and Australia. A mammoth reconstruction and industrialisation programme in Athens prompted another population boom, as people from the islands and villages moved to the city.

Junta & Monarchy

In 1967 a group of right-wing army colonels (the junta) launched a military coup. In their ensuing seven-year reign, political parties and trade unions were banned and opponents were jailed or exiled.

On 17 November 1973, tanks stormed a student sit-in at Athens' Polytechnic, killing 20 students. The US-backed junta's downfall came after a disastrous attempt to topple the Makarios government in Cyprus provoked a Turkish invasion of the island.

Democracy returned to Greece in 1974 and a referendum subsequently abolished the monarchy, which remains in exile today. A dispute between the former king, Constantine, and the government over the family's assets was settled in 2002 and the former royal family now often returns to Greece as private citizens.

Athens Today

Since the 1980s, fundamental social and economic changes have taken place as Greece fast-tracked its development into a modern country, with the most dramatic changes occurring in the '90s and the years leading up to the 2004 Olympics.

Athens has become a more modern, cosmopolitan and wealthy society over the last 20 years, although there are still big social imbalances, and it is in many ways struggling to keep up with itself.

An ambitious infrastructure programme, including the expansion of road and transport networks and the new airport, has made Athens a more efficient and functional capital, though it's still a case study in organised chaos. Billions were poured into city centre redevelopment before the Olympics, and the revitalisation of the city has continued.

ENVIRONMENT

Athens is a hilly city in a basin surrounded by mountains – Mt Hymmetos to the east, Mt Pendeli and Mt Parnitha to the north and Mt Aigaleo to the west, with the Saronic sea to the south. This topography contributes to the dreaded *nefos*, the blanket of smog that can still plague the city. It is far less of a problem nowadays following successful efforts in the 1990s to reduce vehicle and industrial pollution, including restrictions on vehicles in the centre, better public transport, the gradual abolition of leaded petrol and tougher laws.

Athens was significantly cleaned up before the 2004 Olympics, with new waste management systems introduced and a general shift in attitudes to the city's problems.

OLYMPICS LEGACY

The successful staging of the 2004 Olympics changed the image of Athens. Billions of euros were poured into the redevelopment of the city, from new transport infrastructure and stadiums to pedestrian zones around the historic centre. As well, there were major landscaping and beautification projects, such as removing ugly billboards, new pavements, redeveloping parks and squares and the mass planting of greenery.

The legacy of the Games is that Athens today is a radically different city – a more attractive, cleaner, greener and efficient capital, though it is still a work in progress.

The city's spirits and world standing were lifted but it is now dealing with the aftermath of the Games – world-class stadiums and venues for which no long-term planning was done and a hefty €13 billion bill that Greeks will be paying for many years to come.

Millions of trees, shrubs and plants were planted in the Attica area in an attempt to increase green space.

Greece is belatedly becoming environment conscious, with campaigns being implemented in schools. Waste recycling is being slowly introduced.

GOVERNMENT & POLITICS

Since 1975 Greece has been a parliamentary republic with a president as head of state. The president and 300-member parliament have joint legislative power. The left-wing Pasok government of Andreas Papandreou was elected in 1981, the year Greece entered the EU.

Pasok had been in power for two decades (apart from 1990–93) when it was defeated by the conservative New Democracy party in 2004 under the leadership of Konstantinos Karamanlis.

Athens is part of the prefecture (*nomos*) of Attica.

Once the black sheep of the EU, Athens has gained respect for its leadership role in the Balkans, and in 2003 successfully held the six-month rotating presidency of the EU.

In 2003 Cyprus was admitted to the EU, although a settlement on the island's division has yet to be reached. Relations with Turkey remain sensitive but a climate of common cause has led to much economic cooperation and hope for a resolution to the Cyprus issue.

ECONOMY

Greece entered the European Monetary Union in January 2002 and the euro replaced the drachma.

Tighter fiscal policy, structural reforms and a programme of deregulation and privatisation of the telecommunications, electricity, shipping and airline industries have improved Greece's economy.

Economic growth has been outpacing the EU average, with Greece's GDP growing by 3.7% per annum. Growth slowed after the Olympics-related investment boom, but despite spiralling public debt and the Olympics budget blowout, Greece's economy is expected to remain strong.

Tourism is the biggest industry, and the majority of the workforce is employed in services (73.3% of GDP) and industry (21.3%); agriculture contributes only 5.4%.

Parliament (p16) lit up at night

Unemployment is still high (9.9%) but inflation is being contained after dropping from 20% in 1990 to 3.5% in 2006. A late-'90s stockmarket frenzy made many rich, but many ordinary punters lost out in the ensuing crash.

Widespread price rises since the introduction of the euro continue to cause an outcry. Athens is one of the most expensive European cities, despite wages being amongst the EU's lowest. The inexplicable disparity between wages and spending suggests the black economy is still going strong.

SOCIETY & CULTURE

Although there are Athenians of several generations' standing, a large proportion of residents today are relative newcomers to the city, who migrated from other parts of Greece or from Greek communities around the world. Many are descended from families forced out of the Smyrna (now Izmir) region of Turkey in 1923, or who arrived in the 1950s from rural areas.

DID YOU KNOW?
Athens population: 3.7 million
Inflation rate: 3.5%
Greek GDP per capita: US$22,200
Unemployment rate: 9.9%
Number of Greeks outside Greece: 4 million
Number of tourists in Greece annually: 13.5 million

Many Athenians still retain a strong link to their village or island of origin, returning periodically during holidays and on weekends to see parents and grandparents, or to use family properties as holiday homes.

Immigration is changing the demographics of the city and forcing Greek society to confront new social issues. Athens' population of 3.7 million includes more than 600,000 immigrants, both legal and illegal, the majority from Albania, Poland, India, Pakistan and the Philippines.

The city's increasing cultural diversity is becoming apparent in downtown Athens, which has an emerging mini Chinatown, Pakistani hairdressers, Asian food stores and areas where clusters of minorities meet. The growing number of ethnic restaurants reflects both the new communities in Athens and an increasing interest in other cuisines.

But Greece remains largely culturally homogeneous and steeped in traditional customs. Name days (celebrating the saint after whom a person is named) are more important than birthdays and come with

The hubbub of Plaka's (p13) main street

DOS & DON'TS

The Greek reputation for hospitality is not a myth, just a bit harder to find these days in a big and self-absorbed city. Greeks are generous hosts, and guests are expected to contribute nothing to a meal or social gathering. If you are invited out for a meal, the bill is not shared – insisting can insult your host.

Personal questions are not considered rude in Greece, and queries about your age, salary and marital status are considered normal, and opinions expressed freely.

an open-house policy where you are expected to feed all well-wishers. Weddings and funerals are also major events.

Religion remains an important criterion in defining what it is to be a Greek. About 98% of the Greek population belong to the Greek Orthodox Church, though this will change given migrants form nearly one-tenth of the country's population. Most of the remainder are Roman Catholic, Jewish or Muslim. The Greek year is centred around the festivals of the church calendar.

The younger generation of Greeks is highly literate, with a large number studying abroad; a high proportion speak English.

ARTS

The artistic legacy of ancient Greece remains unsurpassed, and is an enduring influence on Western civilisation. People still read Homer's *Iliad* and *Odyssey,* written in the 9th century BC, and ancient sculptures take pride of place in the collections of the world's great museums. Generations of artists have been influenced by the ancient Greeks, from primitive and powerful forms of prehistoric art to the realism of the Hellenistic period that inspired Michelangelo.

Architecture

The influence of ancient Greek architecture can be seen today in buildings from Washington, DC to Melbourne. Greek temples, seen throughout history as symbols of democracy, have been the inspiration for major

You'll lose count of the magnificent columns at the Athens Academy (p33)

architectural movements such as the Italian Renaissance and the British Greek Revival.

One of the earliest known examples of Greek architecture is the huge Minoan palace complex at Knossos on Crete.

In the archaic and classical periods, monumental temples were characterised by Doric, Ionic and Corinthian columns – the Temple of Athena Nike and the Erechtheion on the Acropolis are two examples. The distinct and ornate Corinthian column features a single or double row of leafy scrolls, later used by the Romans, notably on the Temple of Olympian Zeus.

During the Hellenistic period, the main focus was on private houses and palaces, rather than temples and public buildings.

Byzantine churches built throughout Greece usually featured a central dome supported by four arches on piers and flanked by vaults, with smaller domes at the four corners and three apses to the east. The external brickwork, which alternated with stone, was sometimes set in patterns.

After independence Athens continued the neoclassical style that had been dominant in Western European architecture and sculpture, exemplified by the grandiose National Library and Athens University.

Many neoclassical buildings were destroyed in the untamed modernisation that took place in the 1950s, '60s and '70s, when most of the ugly concrete apartment blocks that now characterise the modern city were built.

Many old mansions are being restored as buildings have become heritage protected. Modern architecture is starting to make its mark. The design of the metro, incorporating art and antiquities, has been praised internationally, while innovative restorations such as the old Gazi gasworks complex and Athinais, in an old silk factory, are world class.

Cinema

Greek cinema has for many years been associated with the slow, visual feasts of critically acclaimed director Theodoros Angelopoulos, awarded the 1998 Cannes Palme d'Or for *An Eternity and One Day*. In the mid-1990s, Greek cinema experienced a brief revival, following the moderate domestic commercial success of a number of Greek films. Contemporary filmmakers are producing some worthy films and making some inroads into the international film festival circuit. Two recent films that gained cinematic

ALL ABROAD

Greece maintains strong links with more than four million Greeks living around the world, including an estimated two million in the US and Canada. Many return for annual holidays, own property and are involved in the political and cultural life of the country of their (or their ancestors') birth.

The Greek government has a significant commitment to promoting Greek language, culture and religion abroad and has established a dedicated General Secretariat for Greeks Abroad. Melbourne, Australia, has the third-largest population of Greek-speakers in the world, after Athens and Thessaloniki.

releases internationally were Tassos Boulmetis' *A Touch of Spice* and Pantelis Voulgaris' *Brides.*

Drama & Theatre

Drama dates back to the contests staged in Athens during the 6th century BC for the annual Dionysia Festival. At one of these contests, Thespis left the ensemble and took centre stage for a solo performance – considered the first true dramatic performance and leading to the term 'thespian'.

Thisseion (p94), a little piece of Hollywood

A strong theatre tradition continues today, with the works of ancient Greek playwrights such as Aeschylus, Sophocles, Euripides and Aristophanes performed in the few surviving ancient theatres during summer festivals, most notably at Epidavros and the Odeon of Herodes Atticus. The Greek National Theatre, which stages the pre-eminent performances of ancient Greek theatre, regularly tours internationally and in Greece.

Athens has more theatres than any other European city.

Literature

Pre-eminent ancient poets included Pindar, Sappho and Alcaeus; modern celebrated poets include Constantine Cavafy and Yiannis Ritsos and the two Nobel Prize laureates, George Seferis (1963) and Odysseus Elytis (1979).

The great classical writers included Homer, the historian and anthropologist Herodotus, Plutarch, Pausanias and Thucydides.

The controversial Nikos Kazantzakis, author of *Zorba the Greek* and *The Last Temptation,* remains the most celebrated 20th-century Greek novelist. A spate of translations of modern Greek writers is helping promote the current generation's literary talents internationally.

Music

Athens has a thriving local music scene, but not many contemporary artists or pop acts have made it big internationally since opera diva Maria Callas, living legend Mikis Theodorakis, composer Manos Hatzidakis, Vangelis, Demis Roussos and Nana Mouskouri. A new generation of musicians, however, is starting to make an impact on the world music scene, including pop tenor Mario Frangoulis and vocal artist Savina Yannatou. Many revivalist groups are breathing new life into traditional music and a movement towards *entekno* (artistic or quality) music has spawned a talented generation of singer-songwriters.

LOST IN TRANSLATION

Biblionet (www.gbip.gr) is an online database of Greek books, while the monthly e-zine **Ithaca Online** (www.ithacaonline.gr) is a good resource on contemporary authors and books, and translated Greek literature.

Directory

ARRIVAL & DEPARTURE
Air
Near Spata, the **Eleftherios Venizelos International Airport** (1, C2), 27km east of Athens, is connected to the city by metro, suburban rail link and express buses. Express buses also connect with the ports of Piraeus and Rafina.

INFORMATION
Athens airport has great shopping and services a small museum, on the departure level, displaying archaeological finds unearthed during airport construction. Useful to know:

Airport Information Online (www.aia.gr)
Flight Information (☎ 210 353 0000) All airlines.

AIRPORT ACCESS
The fastest way to and from the airport is by metro or suburban rail. The metro airport service departs from Monastiraki, and you can board at any stop along Line 3. Trains run every 20 to 30 minutes leaving Monastiraki between 5.50am and 9.14pm and the airport between 6.30am and 8.30pm. Tickets cost €6 per person, or for two/three passengers €10/15.

You can take the suburban rail from Larisis and Doukissis Plakentias (Line 3) stations or Nerantziotissa (Line 1). Similar pricing applies.

Airport buses run 24 hours (€3.20, valid for 24 hours on all transport). The X95 airport express bus (5, E4) leaves Syntagma Sq, on Othonos, every 15 to 20 minutes and takes about 50 minutes. Bus X96 (3, C1) leaves Piraeus from Plateia Karaïskaki.

Taxis from downtown Athens take an average of 30 to 40 minutes to get to the airport, depending on the traffic. Expect to pay around €20 to €25, including freeway tolls and baggage surcharge; see also p115.

Bus
International coaches from Turkey, Bulgaria and Albania go to the Peloponnese station, next to Larisis railway station. There are two terminals for **KTEL** (www.ktel.gr) intercity and regional buses.

Terminal A (☎ 210 512 4910; Kifissou 100), northwest of Omonia, has buses to the Peloponnese, Ionian Islands and western Greece. Bus 015 runs from this terminal to Omonia.

Terminal B (☎ 210 831 7096; Liosion 260), 5km north of Omonia, has buses to central and northern Greece and Evia.

Buses bound for most Attica destinations depart from the **Mavromateon terminal** (4, C1; ☎ 210 821 3203; cnr 28 Oktovriou-Patision & Alexandras).

CLIMATE CHANGE & TRAVEL
Travel – especially air travel – is a significant contributor to global climate change. At Lonely Planet, we believe that all travellers have a responsibility to limit their personal impact. As a result, we have teamed with Rough Guides and other concerned industry partners to support Climatecare.org, which allows travellers to offset the greenhouse gases they are responsible for with contributions to sustainable travel schemes. Lonely Planet offsets all staff and author travel. For more information, check out www.lonely planet.com.

Train

International trains arrive at the **Larisis railway station** (4, A1; ☎ 210 529 8740), as do trains from Thessaloniki and the Peloponnese.

The **Greek Railroad Organisation** (OSE; 5, E2; ☎ 1110; www.ose.gr; Sina 6, Syntagma; ☿ 24hr) has another office at Karalou 1 in Omonia (4, B3).

Boat

Piraeus (3, B2; ☎ 210 414 7800) is the busiest port in Greece, with a huge number of departures and destinations, including daily island services. Ferries from Italy dock at Patra in the Peloponnese, and Igoumenitsa in northwestern Greece.

FERRY

Weekly ferry schedules are available from tourist offices, online (www .gtp.gr, or for online bookings www .greekferries.gr) and in the English edition of *Kathimerini* in the *International Herald Tribune*. The main companies are **Minoan Lines** (☎ 210 414 5700; www.minoan.gr) and **Blue Star Ferries** (☎ 210 322 6400; www.bluestarferries.com).

It's best to buy a ticket in advance if you want a cabin or to take a car on board. Otherwise, agents in Piraeus sell tickets (especially around Plateia Karaïskaki). You can also buy tickets on the ferry.

Most ferries heading to the Cycladic, Saronic and Dodecanese Islands and Crete leave from Piraeus or Rafina, while some Cyclades services leave from the recently upgraded port at Lavrio.

HIGH-SPEED CATAMARANS, HYDROFOILS & DOLPHINS

High-speed catamaran or hydrofoil services operate from Piraeus and Rafina and cut travel time by almost half. However, strong winds can lead to cancellations. **Hellenic Seaways** (☎ 210 419 9000; www .hellenicseaways.gr; ☿ 8am-8pm Mon-Fri, 8am-4pm Sat & Sun) has regular services and takes credit-card bookings. Another company is **Blue Star Ferries** (☎ 210 322 6400; www.bluestarferries.com).

Travel Documents
PASSPORT

You need a valid passport to enter Greece (or ID card for EU nationals) and to check in at a hotel or pension.

VISA

No visa is required for stays of less than 90 days for nationals from Australia, Canada, EU countries, USA, Israel, Japan, New Zealand, Norway, Switzerland and most South American countries. Others, and those wanting longer stays, should check with their local Greek embassy.

Customs & Duty Free

There are no duty-free restrictions or sales within the EU. Random and cursory customs searches are made for drugs.

You can bring an unlimited amount of foreign currency into Greece but you can only leave with US$2500 cash (or equivalent). Any more must be in a bank cheque or money order. Importing codeine-based medication is illegal without a doctor's certificate. Dogs and cats must have a vet's certificate.

Exporting antiquities (anything over 100 years old) is strictly forbidden without a permit. It is an offence to remove even the smallest article from an archaeological site.

Non-EU residents can bring 200 cigarettes or 50 cigars; 1L of spirits or 2L of wine; 50g of perfume; 250mL of eau de Cologne; and gifts with a value of up to €175.

Left Luggage

There are lockers at Monastiraki metro.

Pacific Baggage Storage (☎ 210 353 0352) near Exit 1 in the Arrivals Terminal charges €3 to €6 per bag depending on size (six-hour minimum), with varying rates for longer periods.

Pacific Travel Luggage Storage (11, C2; ☎ 210 324 1007; Nikis 26, Syntagma; ☺ 8am-8pm Mon-Sat, 9am-2pm Sun) charges €2 per bag per day, €7 per week, regardless of size.

There are storage lockers at the Omonia and Piraeus metro stations (24 hours €3).

GETTING AROUND

Athens has an extensive and inexpensive integrated public transport network of buses, metro, trolleys (electric cable bus), suburban rail and a tram line. The metro has made getting around the centre of Athens a relative breeze, and further extensions are easing the city's notorious traffic congestion.

The **Athens Urban Transport Organisation** (☎ 185; www.oasa .gr; ☺ 6.30am-11.30pm Mon-Fri, 7.30am-10.30pm Sat & Sun) can assist with most enquiries.

In this book the nearest metro station is noted after the Ⓜ icon; while trolleys and trams are denoted by Ⓣ.

Travel Passes

The €1 integrated ticket can be used on the entire transport network (except airport services) for 90 minutes. The daily €3 ticket and weekly €10 ticket have the same restrictions on airport travel, though it takes a fair amount of travel to make these worthwhile.

Metro

The **metro** (www.ametro.gr) runs from 5am to midnight, every three minutes at peak times, then every 10 minutes. Trains and stations can be a bit stifling in summer as there is limited (or no) air-conditioning. All the stations have wheelchair access.

Travel on Lines 2 and 3 costs €0.80, while Line 1 (ISAP) is split into three sections: Piraeus to Monastiraki, Monastiraki to Attiki and Attiki to Kifisia (one section €0.70). Tickets must be validated at platform entrances. Tickets are valid for 90 minutes and allow connections with trains going in one direction, but you cannot leave and re-enter the station using the same ticket.

Suburban Rail

A fast and comfortable **suburban rail** (☎ 210 527 2000; www.proastiakos .gr) connects Athens with the airport and the outer regions all the way to Corinth. It connects to the metro at Larisis, Doukissis Plakentias and Nerantziotissa.

The suburban rail is expected to extend to Piraeus by 2007 and the ports of Rafina and Lavrio by 2010.

Tram

The **tram** (www.tramsa.gr) that weaves around the coast makes for a scenic journey, but it is not the fastest means of transport. It has services running from Syntagma to Faliro, Syntagma to Glyfada and Faliro to Glyfada. The tram operates from 5am to 1am Monday to Thursday, then 24 hours from Friday night to Sunday, servicing revellers travelling to the city's beach bars. The central terminus is opposite the National Gardens (5, E4). Tickets (€0.60) are purchased on the platforms.

Trolleybus

Athens' overhead cable trolleybuses run between 5am and midnight and service much of the city.

Tickets (per journey €0.50) can be purchased at transport kiosks or most *periptera* (kiosks) and must be validated on board.

Bus

Suburban buses (blue and white) operate every 15 minutes, from 5am to midnight.

Taxi

Athens' yellow taxis are relatively cheap but hailing one can be incredibly frustrating. During busy times, you may have to stand on the pavement and shout your destination as they pass (and they don't always slow down). If a taxi is going your way, the driver may stop even if there are already passengers inside, but this doesn't mean you share the fare. Check the meter when you get in, deduct that amount from the final fare and add the flag fall.

Athens' taxi drivers have a terrible reputation for ripping off tourists and while this is not necessarily the norm, exercise caution in case you land one of the nasty ones (beware, it's often the friendly ones who are the worst). Many drivers smoke in cabs despite an official ban.

Fees should be displayed in the cab and drivers are required to provide a receipt on request.

Flag fall is €1, with surcharges from ports, railway and bus stations (€0.80) and the airport (€3), and for baggage (per item over 10kg €0.30). The €0.32 per kilometre day tariff increases to €0.60 between midnight and 5am (tariff 2). A minimum fare of €2.50 applies.

You can also call a radio taxi (call charge €1.50, or to call and book ahead €2.50). Some companies: **Athina 1** (☎ 210 921 7942), **Enotita** (☎ 8011 151 000), **Ikaros** (☎ 210 515 2800) and **Kosmos** (☎ 18300).

Car & Motorcycle

Driving in Athens can be daunting and frustrating, so visitors are better off avoiding the chaos and parking stress.

Short-term car hire is expensive. Multinationals generally charge more than local companies. The top of Syngrou, off Amalias, is lined with car-rental firms, including **Avis** (☎ 210 322 4951), **Budget** (☎ 210 921 4771) and **Europcar** (☎ 210 924 8810).

PRACTICALITIES
Business Hours

Banking hours are Monday to Thursday, 8am to 2.30pm and Friday 8am to 2pm.

Department stores and supermarkets open Monday to Friday 8am to 8pm, and Saturday 8am to 3pm. Shops usually open Monday, Wednesday and Saturday 9am to 3pm, Tuesday, Thursday and Friday 9am to 2.30pm and 5.30pm to 8.30pm, or 5pm to 8pm in winter. Most major shopping strips in central Athens don't shut during lunch and stay open later; see also p53.

For opening hours for eateries, see p68.

Climate & When to Go

The Mediterranean climate means hot, dry summers and mild winters with bright sunny days. In July and August, heat waves can send the mercury soaring above 40°C (over 100°F), making the city unbearably hot. Balmy summer nights make for lively nightlife, however, and the August exodus of Athenians means it's easier to get around.

Spring and late autumn are the best times to visit. It is pleasantly warm and sunny, the sites and museums are less crowded and you can get some good hotel deals. Winter sees the occasional rainy day (and even exceptional cases of snow) and the city – along with its social and cultural life – takes on a remarkably different character.

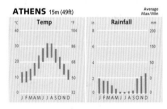

Disabled Travellers

Facilities for the mobility impaired are a recent phenomenon in Greece, fast-tracked for the 2004 Paralympics. Most public building and major museums are now wheelchair-friendly and a special lift even allows access to the Acropolis. Many hotels have upgraded their facilities, the metro has lifts and the airport has excellent facilities.

Making the rest of the city accessible is a monumental challenge. Many museums and older buildings have stairs, most archaeological sites are not wheelchair friendly, public transport can be crowded and restaurants often have toilets down stairs.

Newer buses and trolleys are wider and have seats assigned for those with disabilities, but getting on or off is not easy.

For more information, contact the **Panhellenic Union of Paraplegic & Physically Challenged** (☎ 210 483 2564; www.pasipka.gr; Dimitsanis 3-5, Moschato).

Discounts

Children under 18 and EU students get free admission to state-run museums and archaeological sites (and some private museums), as do classics and fine arts students from non-EU countries. Families can also get discounts at some museums and galleries.

Some private airlines, such as Aegean, offer discount fares to seniors over 65.

STUDENT & YOUTH CARDS

Students with an International Student Identity Card (ISIC) should get discounts to archaeological sites, museums, cinemas and public transport.

SENIORS' CARDS

Card-carrying EU pensioners can claim discounts at museums, cinemas, theatres, ancient sites and on public transport. Others should declare their status, as it is up to the discretion of each institution.

Electricity

Voltage 220V AC
Frequency 50Hz
Cycle AC
Plugs Standard continental two round pins.

Embassies

Embassies in Athens include the following:

Australia (6, C1; ☎ 210 870 4000; Kifisias 1, Ambelokipi)

Canada (6, B2; ☎ 210 727 3400; Genadiou 4, Evangelismos)

Japan (6, C1; ☎ 210 670 9900; Ethnikis Antistaseos 46, Halandri)

New Zealand (6, C1; ☎ 210 692 4136; Kifisias 76, Ambelokipi)

UK (6, A3; ☎ 210 727 2600; Ploutarhou 1, Kolonaki)

USA (6, C2; ☎ 210 721 2951; Vas Sofias 91, Ambelokipi)

Emergencies

Some emergency contacts:

Ambulance (☎ 166)

Fire (☎ 199)

Police (☎ 100)

Tourist Police (☎ 171)

Visitor Emergency Assistance (☎ toll free 112) 24-hour toll-free service; English or French.

Fitness
SWIMMING POOLS

Hotel pools are the only option in central Athens for visitors. Some hotels allow nonguests to use their facilities but at a high cost. Prices normally include a daybed, towel and complimentary drink.

Athens Hilton (6, B3; ☎ 210 728 1000; Vas Sofias 46; Mon-Fri €25, Sat & Sun €45; ᛉ 8am-8pm)

Divani Caravel (6, B3; ☎ 210 720 7000; www.divanicaravel.gr; Vas Alexandrou 2, Ilissia; Mon-Fri €30, Sat & Sun €45; ᛉ 10am-7pm)

Park Hotel (4, D1; ☎ 210 883 2711; www.parkhotel.gr; Alexandras 10, Areos Park; €28; ᛉ 10.30am-6.30pm)

BEACHES

Most beaches close to Athens are organised beaches. There is an entry fee and facilities include sun beds, change rooms, lockers, showers and snack bars, with some boasting tennis courts, water slides, playgrounds and even cabanas for afternoon siestas. Most open 8am to 8pm. There are free beaches at Palio Faliro (Edem), Kavouri and Glyfada. The following organised areas are in order of distance from Athens.

Akti Tou Iliou (1, B2; ☎ 210 985 5169; Mon-Fri €5/3, Sat & Sun €7) At Alimo.

Asteras Beach (1, B3; ☎ 210 894 1620; www.balux-Septem.com; Mon-Fri €6, Sat & Sun €10) At Glyfada.

Thalassi (1, B3; ☎ 210 895 9632; €5/3.50) At Voula.

Yabanaki (1, B3; ☎ 210 897 2414; www .yabanaki.gr; Mon-Fri €5/3, Sat & Sun €7) At Varkiza.

Bus A2 from Panepistimiou (in front of the Academy) stops at Alimo and Voula. To get to Varkiza, get the tram or bus to Glyfada and transfer to bus 115. In summer, express buses go to Varkiza.

GOLF

The only course in town is the 18-hole **Glyfada Golf Club** (9, A1; ☎ 210 894 6820; www.athensgolf club.com; Konstantinos Karamanlis, Glyfada; green fees 9/18 holes €40/52.50; ᛉ 1pm-dusk Mon, 7.30am-dusk Tue-Sun). Call well in advance for weekend bookings.

Gay & Lesbian Travellers

Homosexuality is generally frowned upon in Greece, but there is tolerance of gays and lesbians and a significant closet culture exists.

That said, Athens' has a busy gay scene that is gaining prominence. Gay bars and clubs have traditionally been located around

Makrigianni but a growing number of gay and gay-friendly bars, restaurants and clubs have sprouted in the emerging gay precinct of Gazi.

INFORMATION & ORGANISATIONS

The main gay and lesbian organisation is **Akoe-Amphi** (☎ 210 771 9221). Check out the Spartacus gay travel guide, www.athensinfoguide .com/gay.htm, the limited-English information at www.gay.gr, www .lesbian.gr or look for a copy of the *Greek Gay Guide* booklet at *periptera* (kiosks).

Health
IMMUNISATIONS

No vaccinations are required for entry into Greece. A yellow fever vaccination certificate is required if you are coming from an infected area.

PRECAUTIONS

Health conditions in Athens are generally excellent and tap water is drinkable. In summer drink plenty of water to avoid dehydration and heat exhaustion, and wear sunscreen, sensible light clothing and a hat.

Like anywhere else, practise the usual precautions when it comes to safe sex; condoms are available at pharmacies and supermarkets.

MEDICAL SERVICES

Accident and emergency treatment is available at duty hospitals, which operate on a roster basis. Dial ☎ 1434 to find the nearest emergency hospital, or check the listings in the *IHT/Kathimerini*. A round-the-clock service is provided by **SOS Doctors** (☎ 1016), which charges a fixed rate for hotel or home visits and accepts credit cards.

Travel insurance is advisable to cover any medical treatment you may need while in Athens.

Major hospitals:

Agia Sofia (6, C1; ☎ 210 777 1811; Thivon & Mikras Asias, Goudi) Children's public hospital.

Euroclinic (6, C1; ☎ 210 641 6600; Athanasiadou 9, Ambelokipi) Private hospital.

Evangelismos Hospital (6, A2; ☎ 210 720 1000; Ypsilandou 45-47, Kolonaki) Public hospital.

PHARMACIES

Pharmacists are well trained and licensed to dispense a wide range of medicines that elsewhere only doctors can prescribe. Most central pharmacies have staff that speak some English. A schedule of after-hours duty pharmacies is posted on pharmacy doors, and the *IHT/Kathimerini* publishes daily lists. There's a 24-hour pharmacy at the airport. Or you can dial ☎ 1434 to find a pharmacy.

Holidays
New Year's Day 1 January
Epiphany 6 January
Ash Monday February/March
Greek Independence Day 25 March
Good Friday March/April
Easter Sunday March/April
Labour Day/Spring Festival 1 May
Agios Pnevmatos June
Feast of the Assumption of the Virgin 15 August
Ohi Day 28 October
Christmas Day 25 December
Agios Stephanos 26 December

Internet

There are lots of internet cafés around. You can buy prepaid internet cards at OTE shops or Germanos stores if you've got a laptop.

Most midrange and top-end hotels have internet access in their rooms. Wi-fi access is still rare.

INTERNET CAFÉS
Bits & Bytes Internet Café (5, D1; ☎ 210 330 6590; Akadimias 78, Exarhia; per hr €3; ☻ 24hr) There's also an outlet at Kapnikareas 19, Plaka (11, B1).
Cyberzone (5, C1; ☎ 210 520 3939; Satovriandou 7, Omonia; per hr €2.50, midnight-8am €1.50; ☻ 24hr)
EasyInternet (11, C1; Syntagma Sq; per hr €4; ☻ 8am-3am) Minimum charge to get online, per session, is €1.50.
Ivis Internet (11, C2; ☎ 210 324 3365; Mitropoleos 3, Syntagma; per hr €3; ☻ 24hr)

USEFUL WEBSITES
LonelyPlanet.com (www.lonelyplanet .com) offers a speedy link to many Greek websites. Others to try:
Athens Tourism www.athenstourism.gr
City of Athens www.cityofathens.gr
Greek Travel Pages www.gtp.gr
Ministry of Culture www.culture.gr; www.cultureguide.gr

Lost Property
The 24-hour **tourist police** (☎ 171) can refer you to the appropriate department.

Metric System
The metric system is standard. Like other Europeans, Greeks use commas in decimals and points to indicate thousands. See the conversion table (right).

Money
CURRENCY
Greece adopted the single EU currency, the euro (pronounced 'evro' in Greek) in 2002.

TRAVELLERS CHEQUES
Amex, Visa, Thomas Cook and Euro-cheques are widely accepted but cannot be used as hard currency. You can cash travellers cheques in banks, exchange bureaus and big hotels. **American Express** (11, C1; ☎ 210 322 3380; Ermou 7, Syntagma; ☻ 8.30am-4.30pm Mon-Fri) charges no commission.

CREDIT CARDS
Plastic is accepted in most hotels, retail stores and travel agencies, but not in all restaurants. Smaller retailers often give discounts for cash. To report lost or stolen cards:
American Express (☎ 210 654 7392)
Diners Club (☎ 210 929 0200)
MasterCard/Eurocard (☎ toll free 0080 011 887 0303)
Visa International (☎ toll free 0080 011 638 0304)

ATMS
There is no shortage of ATMs in Athens and most operate in several languages. Some banks around Syntagma also have automatic foreign exchange machines.

CHANGING MONEY
Licensed foreign exchange bureaus can be found around Omonia and

TEMPERATURE
°C = (°F - 32) ÷ 1.8
°F = (°C x 1.8) + 32

DISTANCE
1in = 2.54cm
1cm = 0.39in
1m = 3.3ft = 1.1yd
1ft = 0.3m
1km = 0.62 miles
1 mile = 1.6km

WEIGHT
1kg = 2.2lb
1lb = 0.45kg
1g = 0.04oz
1oz = 28g

VOLUME
1L = 0.26 US gallons
1 US gallon = 3.8L
1L = 0.22 imperial gallons
1 imperial gallon = 4.55L

Syntagma. Banks usually offer the most competitive rates.

Eurochange (5, C1; ☎ 210 522 0314; Omonias 10, Omonia Sq; ☺ 8am-9pm)

Eurochange (11, C1; ☎ 210 331 2462; Karageorgi Servias 2, Syntagma; ☺ 8am-9pm)

National Bank of Greece (11, C1; ☎ 210 334 0500; Karageorgi Servias 6, Syntagma; ☺ 8am-2.30pm Mon-Thu, 8am-2pm Fri)

Newspapers & Magazines

The biggest selection of foreign press publications can be found at the 24-hour kiosks in Omonia and Syntagma, and in Kolonaki Sq.

The English-language papers are the English edition of **Kathimerini** (www.kathimerini.gr) published daily (except Sunday) with the *International Herald Tribune,* and the weekly **Athens News** (www.athensnews.gr). Both publish movie and entertainment listings.

English magazines include the bimonthly *Odyssey* and the monthly city magazine *Insider.* The weekly *Athinorama* is the best source of information about events in the city, but only if you can read Greek – ditto for the free press.

Photography & Video

Most major brands and types of film are available, and many stores do digital printing or can burn photos to CD or transfer to USB drive.

Greece uses the PAL video system, which is incompatible with the North American and Japanese NTSC and the French Secam, unless you have a multisystem machine.

Post

The mail system is quite efficient compared to the old days and while there can still be long queues at post offices *(tahidromia),* at least you take a number and a seat. Many larger post offices have stamp vending machines, fax and courier services. Suburban post offices open Monday to Friday, 7.30am to 2pm. The **Athens Central Post Office** (5, C1; Eolou 100, Omonia) and the one at Syntagma Sq (5, D4) are open 7.30am to 8pm Monday to Friday, 7.30am to 2pm Saturday and 9am to 1.30pm Sunday.

Radio

Athens has more than 20 radio stations, playing everything from jazz and hip-hop to Greek folk music.

Athens International Radio (104.4FM) For visitors and foreign communities, with BBC News.

Cosmos (93.6FM) Pop and rock.

EnLefko (87.7FM) Greek and world music and BBC English News.

Flash (96.0FM) Daily English news bulletins at 9am, 3pm and 8pm.

Melodia (99.2FM) Good mix of Greek and English music.

Telephone
PHONECARDS

There are public phones all over Athens that take OTE phone cards *(tilekarta).* These and many good-value prepaid cards for international calls (€5, €10 and €20) are available at kiosks.

MOBILE PHONES

Greece uses the same GSM system as most EU countries, Asia and Australia. You can buy local prepaid mobile phone cards (that give you a Greek number) at kiosks.

Phones are rented by **Trimtel Mobile Communications** (☎ 210 729 1964; www.trimtel.com).

COUNTRY & CITY CODES

International access code (☎ 00)

Greece (☎ 30)

Athens (☎ 210)

USEFUL PHONE NUMBERS
Duty hospitals/pharmacies (☎ 1434)
International directory & operator
(☎ 161)
Local directory inquiries (☎ 11888)
Police (☎ 100)
Reverse charge (collect) (☎ 161)
SOS Doctors (☎ 1016)
Tourist police (☎ 171)

Television

Greece has several private TV channels. Channel surfing may get you a movie in English, MAD TV music videos or old episodes of US soaps. Otherwise it's mostly Greek soap operas and reality TV shows. The state-run ET 1, ET 3 and NET have quality programmes, documentaries and news in Greek. Satellite TV is available in many hotels.

Time

Athens is two hours ahead of GMT, one hour ahead of Central European Time and seven hours ahead of US Eastern Standard Time. Daylight savings is in effect from the last Sunday in March to the last Sunday in October.

Tipping

Tipping is customary but not compulsory. In restaurants, the service charge is included in the bill, but most people still leave a small tip or at least round up the bill. This applies to taxis as well – a small tip for good service is appreciated.

Toilets

Public toilets are scarce in Athens and keep inconsistent hours, though there are some 24-hour portable, self-cleaning pay toilets (€0.50) around town. The fast-food outlets in central Athens are also handy for travellers. Cafés and restaurants will usually let you use their facilities if you ask politely.

Those little bins in all toilets are for paper waste; never flush toilet paper down the toilet. It's rather third-world and quirky, but helps avoid clogging the system.

Tourist Information

The Greek National Tourism Organisation (GNTO), referred to as EOT (Ellinikos Organismos Tourismou) in Greek, has tourist information offices in Athens and at the airport.

Helpful multilingual staff can provide a handy free map of Athens, the week's ferry departure timetable, public transport information and brochures. You can also pick up a free copy of the glossy *Athens & Attica* booklet.
GNTO (5, E5; ☎ 210 331 0392; www.gnto .gr; Amalias 26a, Syntagma; ⏱ 9am-8pm Mon-Fri, 10am-7pm Sat & Sun)
GNTO airport branch (☎ 210 353 0445; Arrivals Hall; ⏱ 8.30am-8.30pm Mon-Fri, 9am-8.30pm Sat & Sun)
Tourist Police Information Hotline
(☎ 171; ⏱ 24hr)

Women Travellers

Greek men once had a notorious reputation for pestering women, especially foreigners, but the practice (more of a nuisance than an actual threat) is far less prevalent now. Taxi drivers are usually respectful, if grumpy. However, it is always wise to avoid walking in deserted parts of the city and parks at night (especially around Omonia) and to use common sense.

Items for personal and sanitary hygiene are widely available in supermarkets and pharmacies. You can buy contraceptives over the counter.

LANGUAGE

The official language is Greek, but many people, particularly younger folk, speak English.

Probably the oldest European language, Greek has an oral tradition dating back some 4000 years and a written tradition of about 3000 years. Modern Greek developed from a number of regional dialects, mainly from the south. Greek has its own distinctive 24-letter alphabet, from which the Cyrillic alphabet was derived. Transliterations into the Roman alphabet are used in this guide; note that the letter combination dh is pronounced as the 'th' in 'them'.

BASICS

Hello.	*yasas*
	yasu (informal)
Goodbye.	*andio*
Good morning.	*kalimera*
Good afternoon.	*herete*
Good evening.	*kalispera*
Please.	*parakalo*
Thank you.	*efharisto*
Yes.	*ne*
No.	*ohi*
Sorry/Excuse me.	*sighnomi*
How are you?	*ti kanete?*
	ti kanis? (informal)
I'm well, thanks.	*kala efharisto*
Do you speak English?	*milate anglika?*
I understand.	*katalaveno*
I don't understand.	*dhen katalaveno*
Where is…?	*pou ine…?*
How much?	*poso kani?*
When?	*pote?*

GETTING AROUND

What time does the…leave/arrive?	*ti ora fevyi/ftani to…?*
boat	*karavi*
train	*treno*
I'd like a return ticket.	*tha ithela isitirio me epistrofi*
metro station	*metro stathmos*
Where is…?	*pou ine…?*
Is it far?	*ine makria?*
How do I get to…?	*pos tha pao sto/sti…?*

ACCOMMODATION

I'd like a…	*thelo ena…*
single	*mono*
double	*dhiplo*
room with	*dhomatio*
bathroom	*me banio*

AROUND TOWN

I'm looking for (the)…	*psahno ya…*
bank	*tin trapeza*
beach	*tin paralia*
kiosk	*to periptero*
market	*tin aghora*
museum	*to musio*
ruins	*ta arhaia*

TIME, DAYS &NUMBERS

What time is it?	*ti ora ine?*
It's…	*ine…*
today	*simera*
tonight	*apopse*
now	*tora*
yesterday	*hthes*
tomorrow	*avrio*
Sunday	*kyriaki*
Monday	*dheftera*
Tuesday	*triti*
Wednesday	*tetarti*
Thursday	*pempti*
Friday	*paraskevi*
Saturday	*savato*
0	*midhen*
1	*ena*
2	*dhio*
3	*tria*
4	*tesera*
5	*pende*
6	*exi*
7	*epta*
8	*ohto*
9	*enea*
10	*dheka*
100	*ekato*
1000	*hilia*

Index

See also separate subindexes for Eating (p126), Entertainment (p126), Sleeping (p127), Shopping (p126) and Sights with map references (p127).

FEATURES

Mamacas	*Eating*
House of Art	*Entertainment*
Briki	*Drinking*
Orea Ellas	*Café*
Benaki Museum	*Highlights*
Fontana	*Shopping*
Philatelic Museum	*Sights/Activities*
Grand Bretagne	*Sleeping*
Metropol	*Trips & Tours*

AREAS

	Beach, Desert
	Building
	Land
	Mall
	Other Area
	Park/Cemetery
	Sports
	Urban

HYDROGRAPHY

	River, Creek
	Intermittent River
	Canal
	Swamp
	Water

BOUNDARIES

	State, Provincial
	Regional, Suburb

ROUTES

	Tollway
	Freeway
	Primary Road
	Secondary Road
	Tertiary Road
	Lane
	Under Construction
	One-Way Street
	Unsealed Road
	Mall/Steps
	Tunnel
	Walking Path
	Walking Trail/Track
	Pedestrian Overpass
	Walking Tour

TRANSPORT

	Airport, Airfield
	Bus Route
	Cycling, Bicycle Path
	Ferry
	General Transport
	Metro
	Monorail
	Rail
	Taxi Rank
	Tram

SYMBOLS

	Bank, ATM
	Beach
	Castle, Fortress
	Christian
	Diving, Snorkeling
	Embassy, Consulate
	Hospital, Clinic
	Information
	Internet Access
	Islamic
	Jewish
	Lighthouse
	Lookout
	Monument
	Mountain, Volcano
	National Park
	Parking Area
	Petrol Station
	Picnic Area
	Point of Interest
	Police Station
	Post Office
	Ruin
	Telephone
	Toilets
	Waterfall
	Zoo, Bird Sanctuary